Communication for Management
Teaching and Research in Indian B-Schools

Communication for Management

Teaching & Research in Indian B- Schools

Editors

Roshan Lal Raina

Pankaj Priya

Ess Ess Publications

in association with

Lal Bahadur Shastri Institute of Management, Delhi

Published by:
Ess Ess Publications
4837/24, Ansari Road,
Darya Ganj,
New Delhi-110 002.
Tel.: 23260807, 41563444
Fax: 41563334
E-mail: info@essessreference.com
www.essessreference.com

In Association with:
Lal Bahadur Shastri Institute of Management
Shastri Sadan, Sector III,
R. K. Puram
New Delhi-110 022
Tel: 011-26191081, 26172407 Fax: 91-11-26191080
www.lbsim.ac.in

Rs.525/-

First Published - 2007

ISBN: 81-7000-518-3 (10 Digit)
978-81-7000-518-6 (13 Digit)

Printed at Salasar Imaging Systems

PRINTED IN INDIA

Editorially Speaking

The two-day conference on 'Communication For Management: Teaching and Research in Indian Business Schools' saw 14 presentations addressing key issues involved in 'teaching' and 'research' in the field of 'business communication'. The relevance of an appropriate and innovative pedagogy, need for intensive and extensive research and the need to develop business communication as a formal discipline were stressed upon.

An attempt has been made to provide the readers with a brief overview of the various contributions made by the participants, which reflects that the conference achieved it's objectives very well through in depth analysis of the discipline and insightful presentations and the discussions that followed.

The theme address on 'Teaching Communication at Business Schools: The Way Forward 'was delivered by Prof. M. M. Monippally, wherein he stressed on the need to analyse the state of 'communication' in Indian corporate world. He hoped that this conference was the right beginning and forum for discussing these issues.

In the inaugural address on "Value Creation through Effective Communication", A. T. Raman emphasized that knowledge management had become the need of the hour. He highlighted, how effective communication had become imperative for the growth of the global and (specifically) the Indian economy.

'Teaching Persuasive Communication : Reflections on an experimental course for students of management" by M. M. Monippally, Santana Pathak, and Shriti Patra, describes how the authors formulated the course components and adopted innovative techniques to maximize learning. The feedback received from the students at the end of the course acted as an indicator for developing suitable teaching pedagogy for courses that address applied aspects of business communication.

"Business communication : A paradigm shift in pedagogy, delivery, evaluation and feedback, by P. S. Bajaj and M. Gupta, starts with a review of existing models of the communication process. It proposes an alternative model that emphasizes on the role of feedback. The authors advocate that including the element of feedback in the communication loop can do away with the noise factor. They have also described their experience of conducting courses in business communications, the challenges in designing and teaching such courses and difficulties in assessing effectiveness.

'WAC : A teacher's perspective' by Niraj Kumar, outlines the issues faced while designing a customised course for students, finding suitable faculty, the constraints of limited resources, and the importance of developing objective and efficient evaluation criteria. The author has brought to the fore the fact that teaching of business communication, still being in its nascent stage in India, made it all the more difficult for teachers in this discipline to have a standardised framework for curriculum development.

'Communication for management : Teaching and research in the international context' by Abha Rishi, elaborates upon the cross-cultural context and the need to bring in the 'think global, act local' perspective to business communication. She has emphasized on the need for a critical reflexive framework to develop the spirit of exploration, enquiry and creative learning.

'Gender differences in the use of FTAs when reporting incidents of UI : An Indian study' by Esha Patnaik and Asha Kaul, focuses on research in gender communications. Their study reflects on the likely differences in how women and men use face threatening acts while attempting to influence their superiors.

'Leadership communication: Decoding the mystique' by Neerja Pande, while discussing about 'leader profile' makes a case for 'communication' as an effective tool for making a transition from a manager to a leader.

'Reflections on Communication and Extension Courses for Forest and Natural Resource Management' by K. N. Krishna Kumar, is an experience sharing paper on developing specialised courses in communication for students of forest and natural resource management. The concept of offering application-oriented courses in business communication in academic programmes for natural resource management is appealing for its novelty.

'Teaching Presentation Skills : Evaluation of Assessment Parameters in a Class-Room Setting' by Payal Mehra, discusses about her experience of designing and offering a course in business communication, assessing the effectiveness of such a course and gauging the learning and skill development of the students. The focus of the paper has been on the assessment of the presentation skills of the students. A 'before' and 'after' approach of systematic assessment has identified specific skill areas for each student and formed the basis for developing customised intervention strategies.

Informal communication has become so much a part of everyday social and business interaction, but still has been one of the neglected areas of formal research. **'An open eye and ear approach to managerial communication'** By Sharmila Subramanian, has highlighted the impact of informal communication in the workplace, from enhancing mutuality and solidarity to spreading rumours and countering formal networks. The author offers a 'sender-centric approach' to communication that builds on individual capability enhancement.

'An evaluative study of Business Communication Courses Taught in Leading US/UK/European Business Schools, with special reference to Cross-Cultural and E-Business Environment : A Proposal by R. L. Raina highlights the need for studying the evolution of course in the area of business communication in different contexts/countries particularly in terms of the course contents, pedagogy, evaluation mechanism and feedback parameters.

Technology implication in professional communication by Susheel Chabra, brings into focus the ways we can use multi-media and other such technologies for improving the scope and quality of communication. Computer networking, video conferencing, and net-meetings are just indicators of the high-end technological tools that are available for the purpose. However, as technological advancements convert the world into a global village, the fallout is in terms of deterioration in the human component of communication. The author stresses on the need to maintain a balance between the human and the mechanical elements in this dynamic communication environment.

'Teaching communication course/s in business schools : A need of the hour' by Pankaj Priya and R. L. Raina elaborates on a pertinent issue facing academicians in this field today – the gap between the need for an in-depth, formal course in communication and the absence of a structured and specific approach to deliver the same. They have looked into the structure of business communication courses in management schools in the NCR. The study reveals that while institutes offer such courses, the due seriousness which is called for to develop the area as an independent academic discipline is yet to emerge.

We wish our readers a stimulating reading.

R. L. Raina
Pankaj Priya

Contents

Page

Editorially speaking

Theme address
Prof. M. M. Monipally

1. Teaching Business Communication at Business Schools : The Way Forward ... 29
M. M. Monippally

2. Value Creation Through Effective Communication ... 32
A. T. Raman

3. Teaching Persuasive Communication: Reflections on an Experimental Course for Students of Management ... 39
M. M. Monippally
S. Pathak
S. Patra

4. Business Communication : A Paradigm Shift in Pedagogy, Delivery, Evaluation and Feedback ... 55
P. S. Bajaj
M. Gupta

5. Leadership Communication : Decoding the Mystique. ... 89
Neerja Pande

6. Communication for Management : Teaching & Research in the International Context. ... 103
Abha Rishi

7. Gender Difference in the Use of FTAs When Reporting Incidents of UI : An Indian Study. ... 117
Esha Patnaik
Asha Kaul

8. W A C : A Teacher's Perspective. ... 149
Niraj Kumar

9. Reflections on Communication & Extension Courses For Forest and Natural Resource Management. ... 155
K. N. Krishna Kumar

10. Teaching, Presentation Skill : Evaluation of Assessment Parameters in a Class-Room Setting. ... 172
Payal Mehra

11. An "Open Eye and Ear" Approach to Managerial Communication. ... 188
Sharmila Subramanian

12. Teaching Communication Courses in Business Schools : A Need of the Hour. ... 210
Roshan Lal Raina
Pankaj Priya

13. An Evaluative Study of 'Business Communication' Courses Taught in Leading US/UK/European Business Schools : A Proposal. ... 213
Roshan Lal Raina

14. Technology Implications in Professional Communication. ... 219
Susheel Chhabra

Index ... 228

Preface

'A National Conference on Communication for Management : Teaching and Research in Indian Business Schools' was organized by the Lal Bahadur Shastri Institute of Management (LBSIM), Delhi, during March 7-8, 2006. Dr. Roshan Lal Raina, Director of the institute, was the Conference Director. The two-day conference saw 14 presentations that addressed various aspects of teaching and research in the field of business communication. A panel discussion brought up issues facing the field today and outlined scope for future academic development and research in the area.

Day 1: 7th March 2006, Tuesday

The conference activities started on March 7, with registration of the paper presenters, followed by the garlanding of the statue of Shri Lal Bahadur Shastri and screening of a short film on him. The conference commenced with the lighting of the ceremonial lamp in the auditorium. Prof. M Bakaya, Dean (Academics), LBSIM, presented the welcome address in the inaugural session. He spoke about the development of LBSIM as a centre for knowledge dissemination and how communication had played an integral role in its growth. For the participants who had come from institutes around the country, this was a glimpse into the evolution of the institute.

Speaking about how the conference came about, Prof. RL Raina, Conference Director, sketched a vivid picture of how the conference had first started (at IIMA) and the commitment and effort that had gone into reviving the forum after a gap of four years.

The inaugural address was delivered by Mr AT Raman, Project Editor of Business India, Delhi. He spoke on Value Creation through Effective Communication and emphasized that knowledge management had become the need of the hour and effective communication has become imperative for the growth of the global and specifically the Indian economy. He also advocated that skillful management of the intellectual capital of the country could be a driver for growth and for the development of India into a major management hubs.

In his theme address, Prof. MM Monippally, Indian Institute of Management, Ahmedabad, highlighted on key areas for developing the field of business communication. The need for intensive and extensive research, the relevance of an appropriate and innovative pedagogy and the need to develop business communication as a formal discipline were stressed upon.

The thank-you note was delivered by Prof. GL Sharma, Dean (Administration), LBSIM, Delhi.

TECHNICAL SESSION I

Session chairperson: Prof. M. M. Monippally

Rapporteur: Ms. Santana Pathak

The first technical session of the conference addressed a range of issues, from designing a basic course in business communications to offering specialised courses on various aspects of the field. Three papers were presented in this session.

The first paper, titled **'Teaching persuasive communication :** Reflections on an experimental course for students of management ' was presented by Prof. M. M. Monippally, Ms Santana Pathak, and Ms Shriti Patra of the

Indian Institute of Management, Ahmedabad. For a topic that is so much an integral part of everyday managerial interaction, the process of designing a course for it was not so easy. They described how they formulated the course components and adopted innovative techniques to maximise learning. The feedback received from the students at the end of the course were pointers to developing suitable teaching pedagogy for courses that address applied aspects of business communication.

Ms Monica Gupta, Institute of Management Technology, Ghaziabad, presented her paper **Business Communication** : A paradigm shift in pedagogy, delivery, evaluation and feedback' co-authored with Prof. P. S. Bajaj. Starting with a review of existing models of the communication process, she proposed a likely alternative model that emphasizes on the role of feedback. It is proposed that the noise factor can be done away with by figuring in the feedback loop. The concept of having two receivers in the communication process and doing away with noise generated interest in the audience. She also described her experience of conducting courses in business communications, the challenges in designing and teaching such a course and difficulty in assessing its effectiveness.

The discussion on teaching and assessment was carried forward through the paper **'WAC : A teacher's perspective'** presented by Mr. Niraj Kumar of the Xavier Institute of Management, Bhubaneshwar. Based on his personal experience with the course, he shared the issues he faced while designing a customised course for students, finding suitable faculty, the constraints of limited resources, and the importance of developing objective and efficient evaluation criteria. The teaching of business communication still being in its nascent stage in India makes it difficult for teachers in this discipline to have a standardised framework for curriculum development.

TECHNICAL SESSION II

Session chairperson : Prof. Neerja Pande

Rapporteur : Ms Shriti Patra

Focusing on the research aspect of business communication, the second technical session took business communication out of the classroom and looked at it in the organisational context. This session had three papers.

The first paper of the session was by Prof. Abha Rishi, Laxmi Devi Institute for Engineering and Technology, Alwar, titled **'Communication for management : Teaching and Research in the International Context'.** Her engaging presentation elaborated upon the cross cultural context and the need to bring in the 'think global, act local' perspective to business communication. She emphasized on the need for a critical reflexive framework to develop the spirit of exploration, enquiry and creative learning.

'Gender differences in the use of FTAs when reporting incidents of UI : An Indian study' by Ms Esha Patnaik, Indian Institute of Management, Ahmedabad, focused on research in gender communications. She presented the findings of a study conducted by her and her co-author Prof. Asha Kaul that looked into likely differences in how women and men use face threatening acts while attempting to influence their superiors. The audience's curiosity was aroused by the various linguistic approaches managers adopt to influence higher-ups in the organisation.

Dr. Neerja Pande, Indian Institute of Management, Lucknow, through an inspiring presentation on a leader profile, made a case for 'communication' as an effective tool for making the transition from a manager to a leader. She touched a chord with the audience with her insights on how character makes a person. Along with professional achievements, character building is a critical component in being a leader. She drew insights from management, literature and philosophy to elucidate on the traits of a leader and leadership communication.

TECHNICAL SESSION III

Session Chairperson : Prof. K. N. Krishna Kumar

Rapporteur : Prof. Payal Mehra

Innovativeness and experimentation in research and teaching of business communication were central to the four papers presented in this session.

The session started on an interesting note with Prof. K. N. Krishna Kumar, Indian Institute of Forest Management, Bhopal, reflecting on his experience of developing specialised courses in communication for students of forest and natural resource management. 'Reflections on communication and extension courses for forest and natural resource management' addressed concerns of incorporating conservation and livelihood management into a course on communication. The concept of offering application-oriented courses in business communication in academic programmes for natural resource management appealed in its novelty.

Continuing with the mood and tone of the session, Prof. Payal Mehra, from the Jaipura Institute of Management, Lucknow, took the audience through her experience of designing and offering a course in business communication, assessing the effectiveness of such a course and gauging the learning and skill development of students. The focus was on the assessment of their presentation skills. A 'before and after' approach of systematic assessment identified specific skills areas for each student and formed the basis for developing customised intervention strategies.

Informal communication, so much a part of everyday social and business interaction, has been one of the neglected areas of formal research. Prof. Sharmila Subramanian, Institute of Management and Information Science, Bhubaneswar, made us look afresh at this interesting topic through her presentation **'An open eye and ear approach to managerial communication.'** Her engaging presentation highlighted the impact of informal communication in the workplace, from enhancing mutuality and solidarity to spreading rumours and countering formal networks. Prof. Subramanian offered a sender-centric approach to communication that builds on individual capability enhancement. Based on her research in this area, she has proposed an FDP programme on informal communication to be introduced in her institute.

The closing paper of the day, **'Honing communication skills of managers from IIMA : Miles covered and road ahead'** had two young speakers Ms Shilpa Sawant and Mr. Vivek Chauhan from the Indian Institute of Management, Ahmedabad, review the communication courses offered by their institute. The highlight was their exploratory study on the effectiveness of the communication programmes based on feedback by second year students who had returned from their summer internship. Some of the areas where students thought they required more input were giving and receiving feedback, persuasion skills, negotiation, skills in cross-cultural communication, and body language.

Day 2 : 8 March. 2006, Wednesday

The context for the second day of the conference was the current status of business communication as an academic discipline in India. Starting with the technical session to the panel discussion, the agenda was to examine what is happening in the field today, where it stands, and possible directions for the future.

TECHNICAL SESSION IV

Session Chairperson : Prof. RL Raina

Rapporteur : Mr. Pankaj Priya

Sensing the need to focus on current issues rather than

engage in just academic presentations, Prof. R. L. Raina, from LBSIM, Delhi, after presenting his paper entitled 'An Evaluative Study of Business Communication Courses Taught in Leading US/UK/European Business Schools : A Proposal' chose to keep it for discussion and instead take up a more impending issue before academicians – assessing the effectiveness of a course in achieving its desired learning objectives. Musing upon his experience while with the Indian Institute of Management, Lucknow, he spoke of the effort required to make the much-needed transition from information-gathering to knowledge enhancement. Revamping the assessment pattern in communication courses at the institute was at the core of his efforts in this direction. Prof. Raina invited suggestions for further refinement of the evaluation pattern of communication courses.

Mr. Susheel Chhabra, LBSIM, Delhi, brought into focus how multi-media and other such technologies could be used for improving the scope and quality of business communication, through his paper 'Technology implications for professional communication'. Computer networking, video-conferencing, and net-meetings are just indicators of the high-end technological tools that are at our disposal. However, as technological advancements convert the world into a global village, the fallout is in terms of deterioration in the human component of communication. Mr. Chhabra expounded on the need to maintain a balance between the human and the mechanical elements in this dynamic communication environment.

Mr. Pankaj Priya, LBSIM, Delhi, in his paper co-authored with Dr. R. L, Raina, 'Teaching communication course/s in business schools. A need of the hour,' elaborated on a pertinent issue facing academicians in this field today – the gap between the need for an in-depth, formal course in communication and the absence of a structured and specific approach to deliver it. They had looked into the structure of business communication courses in management institutes in the NCR. Their study revealed that while institutes offer such courses, the due seriousness which was called for to develop the area as an independent academic discipline is yet to emerge.

PANEL DISCUSSION

Panel Moderator : Prof. Mukesh Chaturvedi

Panelists : Prof. MM Monippally, Prof. RL Raina, Prof. KN Krishna Kumar, Prof. Payal Mehra, Prof. Sharmila Subramanian

Rapporteur : Mr. Vivek Chauhan

With a panel comprising members from business schools across the country, the issues that emerged during the discussion were diverse. While standardisation of teaching methodologies is important for a formal discipline, the specificity of each institute's requirements has also to be kept in mind while devising innovative teaching methodologies. The panel launched right into the heart of the matter with Prof. Mukesh Chaturvedi, Management Development Institute, Gurgaon, outlining the aspects that we needed to focus on in the field of business communication, namely, teaching, interface with the industry, research in communication and approaches to bridge existing gaps in these areas. Speaking on innovativeness in teaching, he gave an example of how theatre could be successfully used for understanding the process of communication.

The panel deliberated on a host of communication-related issues such as specialised research and development, customising academic courses to address specific needs of students, developing application-oriented competencies in students, having a cross-disciplinary approach in the field of research and teaching of business communication, and developing business communication as a formal academic discipline.

The young students' community attending the conference drew attention to the intellectual capital that is the foundation of our future management expertise. Their enthusiasm, curiosity and insight were infectious. From introducing new courses to transferring theory to practice, they engaged the panelists in an interesting dialogue. The session was a stimulant to the spirit of enquiry and research.

CONCLUSION

The conference set the context for academicians and students alike to deliberate, discuss and develop the discipline of 'business communication' as an independent field of study and academics, and not just as an 'appendix' to other courses in management institutes. The call was to sustain this drive for exploration and innovation. Moving beyond theoretical constructs to applications, from unidirectional transfer of information to knowledge attainment and sharing is essential to build this discipline and make it central to management education and research.

Contributors

Abha Rishi

A Masters in Foreign Trade, International Business and M.Phil in International Business, she shifted to academics in 2004 after working in the industry for over ten years. She has had foreign exposure during her corporate stint. She has presented four papers and attended various seminars, workshops and conferences. She is faculty member at Laxmi Devi Institute for Engineering and Technology, Alwar.

Asha Kaul

A Ph.D. (1990) in Stylistics from Indian Institute of Technology, Kanpur, she has taught at various B-Schools across India after starting her career with IIM, Lucknow in 1983. She has also been a Communications consultant to the U.P. Tourism Department. She has also conducted workshops for companies like KPMG, Motorola, Samsung, Hero Honda, Infosys, etc. Her research areas include gender, social identity and Upward Influence Strategies. She has authored two books on Business Communications published by PHI. She is currently with IIM, Ahmedabad.

Esha Patnaik

She has an education background in the field of psychology and has worked in the fields of journalism, communications and publications. She is currently working as a counsellor at Indian Institute of Management, Ahmedabad.

Krishna Kumar, K. N.

Recipient of ICAR junior and senior fellowship for PG and Ph.D. programmes, he has served as Information Specialist in Tamilnadu Agricultural Department and as Assistant Professor (Agricultural Extension) in Tamilnadu Agricultural University. He worked on the projects on Science and Technology Transfer to Farm Women, Rice bio-technology sponsored by International Rice Research Institute, Philippines and Rockfeller Foundation. Also served as Honorary consultant to M. S. Swaminathan Research Foundation for Bio-village project at Pondicherry. Currently working in projects related to forestry extension and community forestry.

Monica Gupta

Currently working as Associate Professor (HR & Business Communication at IMT Distance and Open Learning Institute, Ghaziabad; has more than 11 years' managerial, teaching and research experience. She has taught courses on Business Communication and Managerial Economics & Economic Environment of India. This includes teaching assignments at M/s GENPACT and ERICCSON and visiting assignment at IILM.

Monica Gupta has done PGDBM from Birla Institute of Management Technoolgy, New Delhi, M.A. (Economics) from Himachal University. She has completed her M.Phil. from BIMTECH and submitted her Ph.D. thesis in Management to Agra University.

M. M. Monippally

A Ph.D. from Manchester University, UK, he has taught at various B-Schools, both within and outside India as a permanent and guest faculty. He has designed and run training workshops in different aspects of managerial communication for middle and senior managers. His current teaching and research interests are in managerial communication skills and strategies, especially bad news delivery and persuasive communication.

Neerja Pande

A Ph.D. in English from Lucknow University, she has been teaching in the field of Communication for Management, International Business Communication. She has conducted research in the areas like Cross-cultural Communication and Communication in Virtual Organisation.

Niraj Kumar

He is a Ph. D. and currently working at Faculty of Rural Management, Xavier Institute of Management. He has published research, review, and concept papers (more than 20) in international and national publications. He has conducted training programmes on Communication Strategies for Natural Resource Management for the officers of state forest departments and for the representatives from NGOs.

Pankaj Priya

An M.B.A. from Birla Institute of technology Mesra , Ranchi, Pankaj Priya has a rich blend of corporate and academic experience. He has spent 11 years in corporate world , where he was involved in hardcore marketing. He is presently pursuing his Ph.D. from IIT Delhi. He has published eight articles in various national and international journals and co-edited a book. He has been a resource person in the MDPs conducted at Central Warehousing Corporation and Construction Industry Development Centre to name a few. He is an Accredited Management Teacher of All India Management Association. He is associated with two prestigious professional bodies namely, All India Management Association and Consultancy Development Centre.

Payal Mehra

An MBA and Ph.D., she is a faculty in Business Communication Area at Jaipuria Institute of Management, Lucknow. She has a teaching experience of 10 years and an industry experience of one year. She has several published papers to her credit. She has conducted a number of workshops focused on developing communication/presentation skills in executives. She has also presented papers at national level seminars. Recently she was conferred with the "Kamla Best Paper Award", given by the ISTD at a grand ceremony at Mumbai on February 11, 2006. Her paper entitled 'Stress Levels in Organizations and Impact on Employee Behavior', published in the January - March. 2004 issue of the Indian Journal of Training and Development (IJTD) was adjudged best paper published during the year 2004.

Roshan Lal Raina

A Ph.D. he is currently the Director, Lal Bahadur Shastri Institute of Management (LBSIM). He has been a professor in the field of communications at IIM Lucknow. He has been heavily involved in conducting management development programmes and workshops. He has been involved in consulting and research assignments awarded by various institutions across the country and abroad.

Shriti Patra

She has done her Masters in the field of English Literature. Her areas of interests are interpersonal communication and children's literature. She is currently working as an Academic Associate at Indian Institute of Management, Ahmedabad.

Susheel Chhabra

Currently working in the area of Information Technology at Lal Bahadur Shastri Institute of Management (LBSIM), Delhi, he holds an MCA, PG Diploma in Planning & Management of Small Scale Industries (PGDSSI), and recently submitted his Ph.D. in the area of e-Business. His research papers have been published in peer-reviewed journals. He has co-authored a book on "Human Resource Information Systems" and completed two research projects on "Internet & Software Piracy" and "Decision Support System for Recruitment & Selection in Software Development Organizations". Currently, apart from teaching in PGDM & MCA programme, he is a Coordinator, IBM Academic Initiative, Deputy Editor, LBS Journal of Management & Research, Member and Editorial Board, "Information and Communication Technologies and Human Development", IGI Global. He has also organized and participated in conferences and MDPs for corporate and Government executives. His research interests include e-Business Model for Government, Management Information Systems, Software Engineering, Computer Networks, and Operating Systems.

Sharmila Subramanian

She combines in her the vividness of corporate exposure and academic experience. She started her stint in the corporate sector by working for the New Indian Express, Bhubaneswar as a trainee in the year 1999. Prof. Sharmila is a Ph.D. in Corporate Interpersonal Communication and a PG in English with Linguistics and Language Teaching as specialization from Utkal University. She has a PG Diploma in Human Resource Development from NIHRD, and a PG Diploma in Journalism and Mass Communication. She is into training and consultancy for organisations like NALCO, UNDP, Coca Cola and Reliance in the field of Human Resource Management and is involved in developing a comprehensive Health Programme for Govt of Orissa and National Rural Health Mission (NRHM). Her areas of research interest include non-verbal communication, pragmatics, discourse and conversational analysis, HR communication, integrated performance management and strategic communication.

1
Teaching Communication at Business Schools: The Way Forward

*M. M. Monippally**

The theme of this national conference on management communication is, as we know, Communication for Management, Teaching and Research in Indian B-Schools. This represents a welcome departure from the 2001 National Conference on Teaching Business Communication, held at Indian Institute of Management Ahmedabad. There was no real theme then; it essentially brought together teachers of business and managerial communication from business schools all over India for the first time and got them to take stock of what they are doing, and to learn from one another.

One complaint that many delegates voiced during the 2001 conference was that business communication was not being taken seriously as a curricular subject at business schools. It was perceived as one of those sets of soft skills that one could pick up on one's own. It did not need tutoring like the hard core subjects and was therefore peripheral to the B-school curriculum. A corollary was that almost anyone could be entrusted with the job of 'handling' communication if at all some students needed it. Not surprisingly, the teachers of business communication felt that they were not

* Professor, Chairperson Communication Area, IIM, Ahmedabad.

being given due respect as professionals.

The delegates confirmed that none of them had specialized in business or managerial communication and that they were from fields as diverse as Marketing, English Literature, Human Resource Management, Organizational Behaviour, and Business Policy. Unlike in the U.S., there was in India no discipline called Business Communication or managerial communication and no one specialised in it.

To complicate matters further, the general impression was that if one could speak and write English clearly and correctly, one was very good at business communication and one could teach it.

The reason we are not getting enough professional respect is that we are not generating enough knowledge in managerial communication. We need to do quality research in managerial communication and show the world that the insights we provide will make their organizations more effective. We need to show them that good business communication goes well beyond speaking and writing articulately.

Along with high quality surveys to document how we communicate in Indian organizations, we need to conduct in-depth case studies of a wide spectrum of successful and unsuccessful managerial communication to generate insights that will help managers.

Fortunately, the current situation is very different from what we found five years ago. The papers being presented at this conference bear witness to the remarkable change. There are papers on leadership communication, gender communication, persuasive communication, etc. This is the way forward.

We need to go beyond bread and butter business communication skills such as making oral presentations and writing reports, letters, email, etc, and look at deeper aspects of managerial and strategic communication. That doesn't mean that these skills don't belong to our domain or that we abandon them. Instead, let these be the manifestations of deeper aspects of management such as negotiating, influencing, leading, inspiring, etc.

I propose that we take the papers being presented at this conference as the starting point for a research programme. Let's do research in managerial communication going well beyond business communication. Let us, for example, study the way top managements in Indian companies (old economy, new economy, manufacturing, services, small, medium, large, regional, national, transnational, family, professional, etc.) communicates with the rest of the company. Does it inspire? How does it communicate and manage change? How does it deliver bad news? How does it persuade the rest of the company? How does it negotiate internally and externally? How does it communicate with different stakeholders? What are the trends in upward communication? What are influencing and negotiating patterns? How do young managers in Indian firms deal with cross-cultural communication challenges?

There is plenty that needs studying. If the papers at this conference are any indication, we have started the process. Now we need to continue it in earnest. We also need to experiment with teaching managerial communication in a wide range of ways. At IIMA, for example, an experiment is currently under way. Instead of being a stand-alone subject, Management Communication is interwoven with the other subjects being taught on PGPX. This helps the communication instructors to demonstrate to the participants the relevance of communication strategies in the running of the organization.

Let's support one another's research in different aspects of managerial communication. Our future as a profession depends crucially on it.

2
Value Creation Through Effective Communication

*A. Thothathri Raman**

INTRODUCTION

The factors that constitute value for a corporate can be varied and some of these may have never been factored in too. While tangible assets and their contribution in terms of direct financial value is easily understood, intangible factors such as people, knowledge and reputation, that underpin the best-performing businesses is often least understood. Factors like intellectual property, brands etc. could often exert greater pressure on performance of a corporation than its financial strength, share of markets, product quality and such other visible aspects of running a business. Besides, project innovation, exchange of ideas, speed of information exchange leading to faster decision making, interplay of personalities and their influence on decisions are factors least understood. And best of all the roles of communication that links most of these factors remains a grey area for most corporations.

'Effective communication gets effective results' is an experience most corporations would endorse without actually giving credit to the communication aspect relegating it as a non-essential expenditure item, best carried out by a

* Consulting Editor, Business India.

group of highly dispensable PR and communication people. Even in the corporate hierarchy, the communication people find themselves close to the bottom of the pecking order. However, this situation is changing in most corporations and the entry of a new class of people called Chief Knowledge Officers (CKOs) with their only skill being knowledge and the way they would communicate knowledge among the decision makers is making all the difference between success and failure of leading Fortune 500 companies. There is now hardly a single company among this lot which does not have a CKO and most also have a strong communication team, whose job often is internal in nature rather than the traditional external PR activity.

Knowledge & Communication

Knowledge resident in the organization or in the individuals holding key positions in the company cannot be exploited unless it is communicated. Therefore, communication becomes a key factor and organizations that are seriously considering knowledge as a factor of production also are serious about investing in communicating that knowledge across the company and outside. The specious link between knowledge and communication is also an aspect of intense debate and research in the knowledge era.

In the 21st century, the corporates around the world are only too aware it is not only the traditional human resource, high quality of inputs, technological processes, well thought out marketing and brand promotion strategies but other aspects like customer relationship management, supply chain management, Enterprise Resource Management (ERP) and Knowledge Management are equally important components of the value chain that leads corporate performance and growth. Also intangibles like Corporate Social Responsibility, Positioning, Economic Value Added (EVA) among others are also being recognized as dynamic components creating value.

Communication, however, has always been treated as an essential function resorted only in times of need and most corporations do not accord the same amount of space for communication as they would give to other aspects cited earlier. Also the inextricable link between knowledge and its communication has not been fully appreciated even in many companies. Leadership in these companies is also not fully sensitive to building sustainable KM and communication strategies in corporations, mainly because the imperatives of using these aids and their real contribution to the value chain of the corporations has not been understood fully by the corporations. There is also scanty and non-existent literature on the subject.

INTANGIBLE ASSETS AND COMMUNICATION

The value of companies has been shifting markedly from tangible assets, "bricks and mortar", to intangible assets like intellectual capital. These invisible assets are the key drivers of shareholder value in the knowledge economy, but accounting rules do not acknowledge this shift in the valuation of companies. Statements prepared under generally accepted accounting principles do not record these assets. Left in the dark, investors must rely largely on guesswork to judge the accuracy of a company's value.

A study comparing market value to the book value of 3,500 U.S. companies over a period of two decades shows the dramatic upward rise in intangible value. In 1978, market value and book value were pretty much matched; book value was 95% of market value. Twenty years on, book value was just 28% of market value. Lev Baruch, an accounting professor at New York University's Stern School of Business, reckons that in the late 1990s businesses invested a staggering $1 trillion per year in intangible assets.

An asset that is not physical in nature. Corporate intellectual property (items such as patents, trademarks, copyrights, business methodologies), goodwill and brand recognition are all common forms of intangible assets in today's marketplace. Intangible assets can often be considered to have indefinite useful lives, while tangible assets such as factories and equipment generally have defined useful lives, after which they are of little to no value to a firm. "Something of value that cannot be physically touched, such as a brand, franchise, trademark, or patent, opposite of tangible asset" (investorwords 2006)

In the book Cracking the Value Code, the authors Richard E.S. Boulton, Barry D. Libert, Steve M. Samek (Harper Collins 2000), highlight the need to acknowledge intangible assets such as leadership, in measuring the value of the corporation. Based on a three-year study of 10,000 companies by Arthur Andersen, the authors have established a sufficient case for treating intangible assets as the means of assessing the real worth of the companies as distinct from the traditional ways of measuring value using the tangible assets. To measure value generation in the New Economy, the authors suggest a new Value Dynamics Framework for measuring the intangibles in corporates. The framework incorporates the traditional categories of physical and financial assets, but also adds three new assets viz. employee and supplier assets, customer assets and organization assets.

Intangible Assets and Communication, a study by authors Hanno Roberts, Ph.D., Peggy Simcic Bronn, Ph.D. and Karl Joachim Breuni of Norwegian School of Management released by the IABC Research Foundation, and sponsored by BIZ360, concluded that in order for organizations to achieve the most value from their intangible assets they must encourage systematic relationship-building and boundary-spanning behavior by everyone in the organization. The challenge for communication managers is to understand how they can contribute to this process.

According to the report, the term intangible assets is

used in financial accounting to denote those production factors, for which a firm can claim ownership, but are not physical properties. They include such things as customer loyalty, brand equity, access to networks, the knowledge and expertise of employees, business processes and intellectual property rights. Together, these 'soft' assets comprise what is known as the knowledge resource of the organization what the organization in totality 'owns' that, together with its financial resources, provides it with competitive advantage.

"Incorporating intangible assets in financial valuation gives firms the ability to capture a wider definition of the organization's resources than just the financial one", wrote the team of researchers from the Norwegian School of Management BI, who were commissioned to work on this study. Intangible Assets and Communication explores the concept of intangible assets and their relationship to communication, including human capital, relationship capital and structural capital.

The review of existing research led to three tools that practitioners can use for assessing their own organization's capabilities to build relationship capital with various stakeholders. Two of the tools are meant for firms to assess their conditions for sharing information - their network competencies, and staffing and systems requirements for information sharing. The third tool illustrates how the firm can express the activities from tools 1 and 2 into financial and nonfinancial measurements.

Real Corporate communication

Knowledge resident in the organization or in the individuals holding key positions in the company cannot be exploited unless it is communicated. Therefore, communication becomes a key and organizations that are seriously considering knowledge as a factor of production also are serious about investing in communicating that knowledge across the company and outside. The specious link between knowledge and communication is also an aspect of intense debate and research in the knowledge era.

In the 21st century, the corporates around the world are only too aware it is not only the traditional human resource, high quality of inputs, technological processes, well thought out marketing and brand promotion strategies but other aspects like customer relationship management, supply chain management, Enterprise Resource Management (ERP) and Knowledge Management are equally important components of the value chain that lead corporate performance and growth. Also intangibles like Corporate Social Responsibility, Positioning, Economic Value Added(EVA) among others are also being recognized as dynamic components creating value.

Communication however, has always been treated as an essential function resorted only in times of need and most corporations do not accord the same amount space for communication as they would give to other aspects cited earlier. Also even the inextricable link between knowledge and its communication has not been fully appreciated in many companies. Leadership in these companies also not fully sensitive to building sustainable KM and communication strategies in corporations, mainly because the imperatives of using these aids and their real contribution to the value chain of the corporations has not been understood fully by the corporations. There is also scanty and non-existent literature on the subject.

Communication is value

Communication lies at the heart of conveying the real value of the intangible assets and even in the case of tangible assets, without the role of communication the real value of the asset would never be conveyed to the end user. The annual reports prepared with a strong communication strategy in mind could convey far more meaning in terms of the corporate government, ethical practices of the company, the compliance track record of the enterprise, the real corporate value the company carries with its customers and its perception of the business environment etc., leading to a greater value perception in the mind of the user about the company in question.

The brand pundits would vouch that it is communication strategy as much as the intrinsic or aesthetic qualities of the end product that often decide the strength of the brand. A poor communication strategy could easily kill the brand or an overkill communication could easily undo a brand.

Even in the case of governments, its effectiveness is often decided by the strategies it follows for effectively communicating its position in each of the development initiatives it may undertake. Taking the instance of AIDS and the recent Bird flu, it can easily be seen that only through effective communication, the government was able to reach to the mass of citizens to sensitize them to act in order to stem the ill effects of the debilitating illnesses. The successful polio vaccine campaign, the earlier successes with stamping out of the Chicken pox, Malaria and Tuberculosis are stellar examples of effective communication strategies of the country.

Conclusion

Communication forms the core in not just conveying information and corporate developments to the stakeholders but it often determines the basic measure of value that could be attached to any intangible assets in an era where corporate competitiveness lies more with the way they manage their knowledge than their financial assets.

3
Teaching Persuasive Communication: Reflections on an experimental course for students of management

*M. M. Monippally**
*Santana Pathak***
*Shriti Patra***

ABSTRACT

Persuasion is such a pervasive and central human process that several disciplines deal with it and conduct research into it. Persuasion is also taught to help people manage their affairs better both as persuaders and as persuadees in several walks of life. Examples include persuasion courses in law, marketing, and advertising. Persuasion also forms part of rhetoric and interpersonal as well as public communication. Not surprisingly, each course focuses on a different aspect of persuasion. Some courses adopt a sure-fire, formulaic approach to teaching persuasion. Some are purely theoretical in orientation.

This paper reviews several courses focusing on persuasion and goes on to examine critically an experimental course in managerial persuasive communication attempted at IIMA during 2005.

* Professor & Chairperson, Communication Area, Indian Institute of Management, Ahmedabad.

** Research Associates, Communication Area, I.I.M., Ahmedabad

KEYWORDS : Business School Curriculum, Persuasive Communication, Managerial Persuasion, Pedagogy, Systematic Managerial Persuasion

Persuasion may be broadly defined as the process of getting others to change their beliefs or attitudes or to do what one wants without coercing them. It plays so fundamental a role in all avenues of life that researchers in different branches of knowledge such as psychology, sociology, political science, law, communication, and rhetoric study it. Advertising, sales, and marketing strategies depend heavily on models of persuasion. Not surprisingly, there is a strong demand for courses and workshops that teach people how to persuade and how to resist unwanted persuasion. Persuasion also forms part of many written and spoken business communication courses in many universities and business schools.

Although superior ability to communicate persuasively is an essential ingredient of managerial success, it has not received the attention it deserves from business school curriculum designers. An Internet search shows very few courses that focus exclusively on persuasive communication for students of management. In this paper, we shall first review a few representative courses on persuasion from different universities and business schools, briefly describe the ingredients of managerial persuasion, and then examine in detail a course on persuasive communication that has been designed and is being run at Indian Institute of Management Ahmedabad (IIMA) for postgraduate students of management.

COURSES ON PERSUASION

University courses on persuasion tend to focus on theory and analysis rather than practice of persuasive skills. University of Texas, for example, offers a course called "Theories of Persuasion" (Cloud, 2003), which introduces persuasion in many different contexts. The objective is to help students "receive persuasive messages with an analytical and critical mindset". Persuasive messages are analyzed in class to understand how influence is exercised in everyday communication settings. The course defines persuasion, looks at its functions, and explains the principles of and approaches to persuasion before it analyses psychological and social theories of persuasion. It also deals with persuasion and the media, and the application of persuasion in politics and society, and its role in social change. The course does not promise to make the students better persuaders. The aim is more modest: sensitization to the process of persuasion.

The graduate course, "Theories of Persuasion", offered by Purdue University's (2004) Department of Communication, also focuses exclusively on social scientific perspectives on persuasion. It surveys research on persuasion with special emphasis on those theories that have had greatest impact on contemporary scholarship on persuasion. The course also looks at persuasion in different contexts such as interpersonal relationships, mass media campaigns, and workplace.

Levine, Fast, and Zimbardo (2004) describe a field exercise that they run at California State University, Fresno, and Stanford University as part of their social psychology course. The course is built around this field exercise in which students willingly become targets of an expert persuader such as a professional salesperson. Students are then asked to analyze their experience systematically using the social-psychology concepts of persuasion they have learned on the course. Before the assignment, they are also warned about common persuasion tactics that they may be subjected to. The objective of the assignment followed by the analysis is to sensitize them to their vulnerability to persuasion and to help them resist unwanted persuasion efforts by others.

Levine (undated) also speaks about a course on "The Psychology of Persuasion and Mind Control" that he has been teaching at California State University, Fresno, since 1984. This course applies the basic principles of the psychology of persuasion and mind control to "a variety of real-world settings, including diverse areas such as salesmanship, advertising, brainwashing, ideological indoctrination, and hypnosis". The course also examines terrorism, the cult phenomenon, and new religious movements.

According to Stowe (undated), the objective of the course entitled, "Spoken and Written Discourse" that she teaches at Faculty of Communication & Culture, University of Calgary (summer 2005), is to make students better communicators through writing and speaking. The course explores the principles of persuasive communication as seen in "classical rhetoric, essays, newspaper editorials, songs, speeches and debates". The course shows students how persuasion works and what makes one a persuasive speaker or writer.

The objective of "The Power of Persuasion", a course offered by DePaul University School for New Learning, is to help students understand "how persuasion and persuasive techniques can be used in the communication process of relationships, in the family, and in the world of work". (Kurtz, 2003). The methodology is largely analysis of persuasive texts and speeches through lectures and discussions, readings, work in small groups, and an individual project. It is clear from the detailed course description that the focus is not exclusively on persuasion.

Temasek Polytechnic (undated), Singapore, offers a course entitled "Persuasive Communication". According to the school's website, the focus of the course is on the fundamentals of speech communication and presentation skills. It covers activities like oral presentations, report writing, speech writing, and personal grooming.

Courses on persuasion taught in law schools tend to focus largely on logical persuasion achieved through both writing and speaking. University of Maryland School of Law (2005), for instance, has a course called, "Advanced Legal Writing Seminar: Theory and Practice of Persuasion". It draws on classical rhetoric, psychology, and literary theory but focuses on persuasive writing techniques in the context of legal arguments. On the course students both critique and generate legal documents including judicial opinions and appellate briefs. They also critique oral arguments. Students are evaluated on persuasive written documents that they create, critique of legal texts, and reflective essays they write on their own work. There are also non-graded group exercises.

University of Houston Law Center's (Undated), "Attorney Communication & Persuasion Techniques" aims to help students become "more effective, precise, clear, credible, and persuasive". The focus is on psychology of the communication process. (In fact, the earlier title of the course was "Psychology of Communication".) Neuro-Linguistic Programming (NLP) forms the theoretical base of this course.

When one looks at the teaching of persuasion in business schools, the practical orientation becomes evident. Based on a survey of the teaching of persuasion in thirty top ranked business schools in USA, Netzley (2002) says that persuasion theories are not taught actively there mainly because MBA students prefer immediately applicable techniques and because there is not enough time (p 57-58). Besides, persuasion usually forms part of a larger course such as Business or Managerial Communication, Organizational Communication, Marketing, Advertising, and so on. Netzley (p 61) finds that logic is the most important criterion used by business school faculty to evaluate persuasiveness in assignments and that classical rhetoric is unquestionably the dominant theoretical basis for teaching persuasion" (p112).

It is noteworthy that according to Netzley's survey, "59% of the [teachers] dedicate atleast one class, if not an entire module or complete course, to persuasive instruction" (p 73). While this stresses the fact that persuasion is taught widely, it also underscores the observation that there are very few business school courses that focus exclusively on persuasion. Netzley goes on to say that "mere technique or skills instruction that does not lead to comprehending a basic underlying theory is likely to be nothing more than a quick-fix workshop yielding marginal improvement" (pp 75-76). Many executive education programmes might attempt precisely that.

"Sales, Persuasion, and Influence", the course that Pérez-Reyes (1998a) teaches at Haas School of Business Administration, University of California, Berkeley, promises to help the students learn practical persuasive techniques, refine their oral and written communication skills, examine how people are influenced and manipulated by others, and the ethics of persuasion. Students are expected to write an essay on the ethics of advertising, create advertisements and brochures, prepare a three-page policy recommendation, make a sale, and develop a group presentation. This course appears to be attempting a mix of theory and practice of persuasion. At Haas School, Pérez-Reyes (1998b) also teaches "Business Communication BA100", which has some persuasion components along the same line.

UQ [University of Queensland] Business School's (2005) course, "Influence and Persuasion," however, is different from the American ones Netzley has reviewed. Here the focus is more on analysis of persuasion than on practice of persuasion. It enables the students to understand power and influence and analyze the practices of persuasion and influence used by the media. One of the objectives is to help students to reason logically and to detect fallacies. Another is to improve their communication skills. The teaching methodology consists of lectures, presentations by students, and workshops.

THE CHALLENGES OF MANAGERIAL PERSUASION

Is managerial persuasion different from other kinds of persuasion? If yes, in what sense? Does it need to be taught differently from other forms of persuasion?

Persuasion is persuasion, irrespective of the field in which it is exercised. It should be possible to capture the basic principles underlying effective persuasion and teach them. In fact, theories of persuasion try to do precisely that. Need managers be taught differently from others?

Managers and students of management need a different fare from most others interested in learning to refine their persuasive skills mainly because they have to persuade a bewildering array of people - individuals and groups - people with often conflicting interests and orientations: subordinates, colleagues, bosses, customers, suppliers, competitors, and even regulatory bodies. Neither sound theory nor a formulaic approach on its own is likely to give them the insights they need to effectively persuade such a range of people.

First, let's take theories of persuasion. A course that focuses on theories of persuasion does give the learners insights into persuasion and enhances their knowledge levels. It helps them analyze persuasion efforts and indicate why some failed and some succeeded. It may also help them predict whether certain attempts are likely to fail or succeed. It may not, however, make them better persuaders. A knowledgeable literary critic may be able to judge a poem well and explain convincingly why it is good, bad, or great. He/she may not, however, be able to create poetry. Managers are like poets, playwrights, actors, and dancers, not like critics. They are performers, not analyzers. Not surprisingly, managers are impatient with theory and want what they can apply immediately, as observed by Netzley (2002, p 57-58).

Then, how about a formulaic or rubric-based approach to teaching persuasion with minimal theoretical inputs? It will help one deal with well defined persuasion challenges. Salespersons may, for example, be trained to categorize their prospects and choose one of a few pre-determined sets of techniques to persuade them to buy goods or services. This is rather like the training of car mechanics. They may not understand the principles of internal combustion but may be trained to follow a particular routine and swiftly identify what is wrong with a car and mend it. They may do that job faster than an automotive engineer.

Without taking away anything from the tremendous persuasion skills a salesperson needs, or the diagnostic skills a car mechanic needs, one can say that the managerial challenge is much tougher. How should managers prepare themselves to take on the multi-faceted persuasion challenges of managing? Formulaic persuasion may work with some stakeholders but may fail miserably with others. Sound theory may be useful in analyzing persuasion successes and failures, but managers need to perform. Managers need a vibrant marriage of theory and practice, a balanced diet of analysis and action, so that each one can identify their strengths and weaknesses, and arrive at their own heuristics to deal successfully with moving targets. Among all the courses reviewed above, the Haas School course, "Sales, Persuasion, and Influence" (Pérez-Reyes,1998a) comes closest to this idea of a balance between theory and practice.

'PERSUASIVE COMMUNICATION' AT IIMA

'Persuasive Communication', a one-credit (25 contact sessions) elective course tried out on the Post Graduate

Programme (MBA) at Indian Institute of Management Ahmedabad (IIMA) during 2005-06 was an attempt in the direction of combining theory and practice in a dose that is suitable for students of management.

Course objectives: The course had set itself five objectives.

- Help the students understand the process and features of persuasive communication
- Equip the students to discover their own potential and style
- Enhance their repertoire of persuasive communication techniques
- Render their oral and written communication generally more persuasive
- Enable the students to understand propaganda and deception, and resist undue persuasion.

Participants: Enrolment was restricted to 24 students including four Europeans on exchange from other business schools. The class was divided into four groups, each of which was further subdivided into two. In order to ensure cultural, gender, and educational diversity and learnings from it, each of these four groups was required to have at least one exchange student, one student of agri-business, and at least one woman.

Pedagogy: Theory and practice were combined in each session in different and interesting ways. Article reviews, discussion of theory, roleplays, analysis of roleplays, stories, cases, and clippings from feature films, and presentations on great persuaders from history or fiction formed the mainstay of the pedagogy. There was very little teacher-talk. Nearly all the activities were conducted within and between the groups, which also competed among themselves for the Best Persuader Award at the end of the course.

Contents and Structure: Each session started with one

of the students sharing with the class a persuasion-related joke, cartoon, personal experience, or film clip. This, combined with a diary-cum-scrapbook on persuasion everyone was required to maintain during the course, got students to look around everywhere (stories they read, films they watch, interpersonal or commercial interactions they get into, advertisements that they notice, etc.) specifically for instances of persuasion.

Most class sessions had a critical review of a pre-selected article on persuasion by a pair of students and a whole class discussion on the article's contribution to the understanding of persuasion. Through these the class was exposed to the three Aristotelian persuasion factors (ethos, pathos, and logos) and the more recent treatments of persuasion including cognitive dissonance theory and language expectancy theory. This process led to the formation of an increasingly refined shared theoretical framework which would enable the participants to analyze persuasion attempts confidently. This came in handy when each of the four teams had to make a major, 40-minute multimedia presentation on a 'great persuader' from history or fiction and answer questions from the audience.

The students were asked to try their hands at persuasion – planning and execution of persuasion as well as being persuaded – through a range of roleplays. The teams responsible for the roleplay had to plan in advance and execute their plans in class. Role-plays were supplemented with analysis of persuasion-centred cases, stories, speeches, emails, and clips from feature films.

Topics covered in the course included, among other things, bad news delivery, propaganda, and deception. One session devoted to interaction with a Master Persuader. The objective was to give the students an opportunity to interact closely with a master of persuasion and to gain practical tips on persuasion.

Another critical and highly admired component of the course was a live project. Each pair of students had to persuade someone to do something out of the ordinary. (One highly ambitious pair tried - alas unsuccessfully- to persuade AR Rehman to come to IIMA and perform free at its international Business School Meet, 'Confluence'.) Eight pairs chose direct marketing projects in which they had to generate persuasive letters to be sent out to a wide range of readers. Their outputs were graded by the direct marketing companies. Each pair had to make a presentation to the class on what persuasive strategies they adopted for their projects and why. Even failures to persuade were sources of great learning.

Evaluation: Another important aspect of the course was that both the instructor and the students evaluated the reviews, role plays, and presentations. This not only enhanced student involvement in classroom activities but also heightened everyone's awareness about persuasion. The instructor's initial apprehension that students might rate their class mates over-generously and thus vitiate grading turned out to be baseless. The course-end examination (worth 30 per cent of the total weight) focused on application of learning from the course.

STUDENT FEEDBACK

At the end of the course the students gave their anonymous, written feedback, as they do at the end of every course at IIMA. According to this feedback, collected directly by the Administration, the students said that the course helped them understand the subject matter effectively (mean score: 8.86/10) and that the course achieved its stated objectives (mean score: 8.45/10). They affirmed that the interactive processes of the course (eg. class participation and presentations, group discussions, project) were helpful towards learning from the course (mean score: 9.18/10). They agreed that all things considered, the course was excellent (mean score: 8.95/10).

Three months after the course was over, the same students were sent a short questionnaire by the instructor seeking their feedback on the course. Of the 24 students, nineteen (82.6%) responded to the questionnaire. Here are the five questions and a summary of the answers.

1. Why did you take this course? Mention the TWO most important reasons

The overwhelming majority (89.4%) said that they opted for this course as they thought that they needed to refine their persuasive skills for managerial success and this course would help them do so. Twenty-one per cent took the course because they found the course description very persuasive; another 21% took it because they liked the mixture of theory and practice that the course promised.

(The percentages add up to more than 100 because for this and three other questions the respondents were expected to give two answers.)

2. What parts of the course did you find most useful? Choose the TWO most important ones

The blending of theory, case/film analysis, roleplay, project, and games rather than focusing exclusively on theory or practice was, for 78 per cent of the students, among the most useful aspects of the course. This clearly indicates that students of management want a combination of both theory and practice.

Thirty-six per cent considered the live persuasion project the most useful part. A little over one fourth of the respondents rated feedback given by the instructor on the students' persuasion attempts in the class as the most useful aspect of the course. That a smaller proportion of students also rated as most useful the other components of the course such as roleplays (15.7%), analysis of cases and stories (15.7%), face-to-face meeting with a master persuader (10.5%), multimedia presentations on great persuaders (5%) and analysis of persuasive e-mails, further suggests that students of management appreciate a combination of theory and practice.

The only major part of the course that none rated among the most useful was article review, the part that focuses exclusively on theory.

3. What are your disappointments, if any? Choose the TWO most important

Almost two-thirds (63%) thought that the role-plays were not very helpful as no one took them seriously. Similarly, almost one third (31%) found the analysis of stories and cases shallow. There were also some (21%) who thought that there was not enough exposure to theories of persuasion and an equal number (21%) that felt that the course did not equip them enough to resist persuasion.

The answers underline the need to invest more in role-plays and analysis of cases and stories. The disappointment is not about role-plays and analysis of cases as such, but about the lack of depth and seriousness.

4. Please indicate the TWO most important learnings from the course

For almost two-thirds of the students (63%) the main learning is that that good persuasion needs a lot more than logical arguments. A similar number of students (58%) think that the course has enabled them to plan and execute their persuasion plans more systematically than before. Over one third (37%) think that now they can resist unwanted persuasion better. Related to this is the statement by 21 per cent that now they can detect propaganda and deception more easily. One person thinks that meeting the master persuader was one of the great learnings from the course.

The wide range of items being chosen by different students as among the most important learnings from the course also supports the contention that students of management want an integrated approach to teaching persuasion. They are interested in planning persuasion systematically. They can do it only when they are equipped with the right theory and their persuasive skills are honed through meaningful exercises.

5. If we consider managerial persuasion to be an ability to persuade a wide range of stakeholders (bosses, subordinates, peers, customers, suppliers, etc.) using a wide range of approaches (emotional, logical, and ethos-based and a combination of two or more of these) intelligently, how well do you feel PC [Persuasive Communication] helped you acquire it?

Three-fourths (73.5%) of the students think that PC helped them acquire the persuasive skills essential for managerial persuasion. About one-fourth (21%) think the course helped them a great deal. Five per cent thinks that the course did not really help in acquiring these skills. This is in line with the level of satisfaction the students registered at the end of the course through the official feedback, already summarized above.

SUGGESTIONS FOR FURTHER WORK

Based on the feedback from the students who attended PC at IIMA, it can be concluded that there appears to be good demand for courses in managerial persuasion that combine theory and practice through a variety of activities including explorations in the theories of persuasion down the ages and from different disciplines. Exclusive focus on theory may not interest students of management; neither will formulaic practice with little theoretical understanding. Some may be born persuaders capable of choosing the right strategy for every situation they find themselves in; but students of management should learn to persuade systematically because they need to persuade a wide range of people; both theory and practice are equally important in systematic managerial persuasion. The challenge of course designers and instructors is to find a good blend of theory and practice that involves them completely and helps them develop their own heuristics.

REFERENCES

1. Cloud, D. (2003) Theories of Persuasion. Retrieved January 2, 2005 from http://uts.cc.utexas.edu/~dcloud/persuasionsyll2003.htm
2. Kurtz, J. (2003). The Power of Persuasion. DePaul University School for New Learning. Course HC 320. Retrieved January 15, 2006 from www.snl.depaul.edu/searchAdmin/syllabi/HC_320.doc
3. Levine, R. V., Fast, N. & Zimbardo, P. (2004). The power of persuasion - A field exercise. Teaching of Psychology. 31(2), 136-138. Retrieved December 21, 2005 from: http://psych.csufresno.edu/koswald/rlevine/TOP%20article.pdf
4. Levine, R.V. (undated) Courses: Retrieved January 11, 2006 from http://psych.csufresno.edu/levine/teaching.html
5. Netzley, M. A. (2002). Persuasion theory's pedagogical turn in ranked MBA programs. Unpublished Ph.D. thesis, University of Minnesota. Publication Number AAT 3037485, Proquest: http://proquest.umi.com/
6. Pérez-Reyes, A. (1998a). Sales, Persuasion, and Influence. MBA course at Haas School of Business Administration, University of California, Berkeley. http://faculty.haas.berkeley.edu/perezre/unix/BA196_Syllabus.html
7. Pérez-Reyes, A. (1998b). Business Communication BA100. MBA course at Haas School of Business Administration, University of California, Berkeley. Retrieved January 14, 2006 from http://faculty.haas.berkeley.edu/perezre/unix/BA100_Syllabus.html
8. Temasek Polytechnic (undated). ECM1008 Persuasive Communication. Retrieved January 18, 2006 from http://www.tp.edu.sg/courses/synopses/BUS.htm
9. University of Houston Law Center (Undated). Attorney Communication & Persuasion Techniques. Retrieved January 18, 2006 from http://www.law.uh.edu/litigation/
10. University of Maryland School of Law (2005). Advanced Legal Writing Seminar: Theory and Practice of Persuasion. Retrieved

January 18, 2006 from http://www.law.umaryland.edu/course_info.asp?coursenum=588D

11. UQ [University of Queensland] Business School (2005). ORGC2601 Influence and Persuasion (Ipswich). Retrieved January 16, 2006 from http://www.business.uq.edu.au/courses/orgc2601_ipswich/ORGC2601_Course_Outline.pdf

12. Purdue University (2004). Theories of Persuasion. Graduate course details Retrieved January 12, 2006 from http://www.cla.purdue.edu/academic/comm/pdf_doc_etc/Fall_2004_Grad.doc

13. Stowe, L (undated). Spoken and Written Discourse. Communications Studies, University of Calgary. Retrieved January 11, 2006 from http://www.comcul.ucalgary.ca/Web/outlines/data/f01/coms-361-01f-04.html

4

Business Communication a Paradigm Shift in Pedagogy, Delivery, Evaluation and Feedback

*P. S. Bajaj**
*Monica Gupta**

"Some things are so simple and so obvious, but unless they are stated, they aren't necessarily obvious. The obvious can be so simple" — Carol Lynn Nute

ABSTRACT

The first thing that a new born learns is to communicate its displeasure on being exposed to the world from the warm comforts of the mothers' womb. The first and the foremost learning experience after birth is to communicate ones needs, requirements, and emotions. The circle of communication increases with age, education, employment and other social engagements. As the network expands so does the need, degree of sophistication and the influence of communication broadens. Thus the importance of effective communication increases exponentially with the increase in these parameters. But the difficulty of ensuring effective communication increases manifold for managers because

* Chairman DDE & El Ltd. and Professor HR and Business Communication, Institute of Management Technology, Ghaziabad

* Faculty, HR and Business Communication, IMT, Ghaziabad

the corporate communication is in English. English being an acquired language and not mother tongue for most Indians, poses problems of fluency. As Khandwalla, notes in the foreword to the book by Matthukutty M Monipally on business communication strategies, "I have come across far too many young men and women, and indeed older people, who are unable to do justice to their talents because of their disability in communicating effectively. They go through life facing yawns, shirks of shoulders, and other responses that convey boredom, confusion, or irritation in their communicatees. This, of course, is not all. Even good communicators can misunderstand or misinterpret what is intended and land into a soup." With globalization the issue is further complicated as a manager is not only to deal with home land culture but has to grapple with the diverse international cultures. The impact of globalization is two fold – multicultural workforce and global market. As educators our endeavor is to equip the students with the skill and ability to address these issues with confidence and finesse. In fact, when we attempt to design the curriculum of business communication for MBA students, another element enters the list of variables. The intake of most of the reputed management institutes is from all over India and may include a few foreign students. The acumen and degree of fluency with English language of these students is highly diversified. The course design should have inbuilt absorption for these differences. Through this paper we intend to evaluate the existing curriculum of business communication and suggest modifications to make it more suitable for the ever evolving business environment. The paper is divided into four parts. The first part evaluates and suggests strategic course outline giving market-need based practical input. We live in an era when the written and the spoken word – and the gesture – have become alarmingly important: they can make or break careers, contacts, and credit in the market place. Good communication can galvanize effective action and cooperation. Bad communication can breed resentment and resistance. Business communication is serious but need not be dull. Well-turned but appropriate phrases and words can buoy up communication that is otherwise likely to sink into the oblivion of files and waste paper baskets. The traditional manner of teaching is inadequate for the dynamic and ever evolving course on business communication. The primary reason being that the fast paced changes in technology are followed closely by changes in the way people communicate and understand each other. Thus, the second section delves on a delivery mechanism with a difference. Unlike other management courses business communication is purely practical in nature and is needed at all times during the waking hours. Business communication is cultivated communication. It needs to be strategic in the sense of a healthy, long term relationship between the communicator and the communicatee. Therefore, it becomes imperative to measure the effectiveness of the course in ensuring development of communication skills in conjunction with industry requirements. The course needs to be continuously reinforced based on feedback received from students and industry. Thus, the third section develops the feedback and evaluation systems pedagogy to include both students and industry. The course once developed should be capable of continuously evolving with the changes in business environment and business structures. The course should be dynamic, immediately responding to the fast track changes in the business environment strengthened by the technological revolution. In view of this, in the fourth section we attempt to suggest a course curriculum updation mechanism – Kaizen Teian.

KEYWORDS : Business Communication, Pedagogy, Delivery, Evaluation, Feedback.

INTRODUCTION

Effective communication skills form the nucleus around which all successful human relations revolve. Whether we are sitting, walking, talking, listening or thinking, we are engaged in some form of communication. This could be verbal or non-verbal. All these channels of transmitting messages are equally important and need to be analyzed in order to master the art of effective communication. An in-depth study of the nuances of communication provides an insight into the nature of the human mind and the resultant behavior and prompts us to raise a few queries: what makes an individual respond in a particular manner and to a specific situation? Is his style of communication a reflection of his personality? If so, would an understanding of the art and science of communication help him to become an effective communicator? The answers to these questions form the crux of the study of interaction (Kaul, 2001).

SECTION I : STRATEGIC COURSE OUTLINE

Today, communication has become an integral part of our life. Inability to communicate effectively and efficiently can jeopardize our interests in business and other managerial functions, especially controlling and organizing. Be it interpersonal or intrapersonal relationships, the role of communication cannot be underestimated. However, the perception of business communication as a subject is still low in terms of academic importance. It is widely perceived by the students as not as difficult as quantitative techniques or financial management. Many management institutes are trying to bridge the gap by giving communication skills more importance in their curriculum design, but still much needs to be done to give managerial communication its rightful due (Mehra, 2005). The significance of communication can be gauged by the fact that whenever there are impediments in the communication process, the flow of activities loses its momentum and misunderstandings may crop up resulting in failure of relationships and situational breakdowns. Understanding how communication works in business and how to communicate competently within an organization helps in participating in every aspect of business. Consider these recent research findings - all of which come from studies conducted in the 1990s and beyond (Ober, 2005):

- Research conducted in USA in 2000 by National Association of Colleges and Employers (NACE) identified top ten characteristics employers seek in job candidates. Number one was communication skills, followed by motivation/initiative and teamwork skills.
- A survey of 224 recent business graduates ranked communication as the most important area of knowledge both for securing and for advancement and promotion once on the job.
- A survey of 6000 people conducted by Young Executive magazine found that the most annoying habit of American bosses was poor communication.
- A survey of 200 corporate vice-presidents reported they spend the equivalent of nearly three months a year writing correspondence and reports.
- A survey of 1,000 white and blue-collar workers found that the most frequent cause of workplace resentment and misunderstandings is poor communication.
- Eighty per cent of the managers at 402 firms surveyed nationwide said that most of their employees need to improve their writing skills, up from 65% the previous year. But only 21% of the firms offered training in writing skills.

Clearly, good communication skills are crucial to success in organizations.

The primary objective of business communication course is to introduce the concept and essential elements of communication. The simple premise that underlies the paper is that if the basic skills can be grasped and then honed, they would bring about transformation in an individual's communicative abilities. Excellent oral communication skills are considered to be the highest trait for becoming a successful manager and this is the basic concern of the corporate bosses as well students of management courses to achieve milestones in their career. The motivation behind this work is to present a comprehensive course outline which would cover essential topics for Business Communication.

WHAT IS COMMUNICATION?

Communication can be considered as a personal process that involves the transfer of information and also involves some behavioral input. Communication is something people do. It can be very complex or very simple; very formal or informal – it all depends on the nature of the message to be passed, and on the relationship between the sender and the receiver (Ludlow and Panton 2002).

It consists of the transfer of information and understanding between parts and people in an organization, and the various modes and media involved in communication interchanges. Effective communication, therefore, is critical to the success of an organization.

Let us look at the changes that are occurring in organizations today:

- Structure and technology are becoming more complex in organizations.
- Economic and market conditions are forcing greater efficiency and quality in manufacturing and services.
- Customers are looking for customized products and solutions demanding greater involvement and interaction.
- Government legislation requires managers to interpret the changing implications for policies and practices in their own organization.
- People at work, especially the younger ones, are expecting more from their employers – not just higher wages, but also greater personal and job satisfaction. The index for evaluation is the level of quality of life.
- They are becoming more dependent on horizontal

communication channels. With increased complexity, information needs to flow quickly between specialists rather than go up and back down the hierarchy, with its inevitable delays and message distortion.

So when we look at the changes that are taking place in organizations today, it is clear that managers, to be effective, require communication performance at hitherto unheard-of levels of excellence.

Some of the common answers to the question 'why communicate?' are as follows:

– It leads to greater effectiveness.
– It keeps people in the picture.
– It gets people involved with the organization and:
  * Increases motivation to perform well;
  * Increases commitment to the organization.
– It makes for better relationships and understanding between:
  * Boss and subordinate;
  * Colleagues;
  * People within the organization and outside it.
– It helps people to understand the need for change:
  * How they should manage it;
  * How to reduce resistance to change.

COMMUNICATION PROCESS MODEL

Aristotle's Model

It was Aristotle in his Rhetoric who first gave the science a proper framework. He proposed a simplistic model of communication which had as its components, a sender a receiver and a message. It forms the crux around which the later theories were formulated. Aristotle emphasized the persuasive tactics used by the sender in bringing about a change in the thinking process of the receiver. In this model the source or the sender was of primary importance. The process of communication was one-way (Kaul, 2001).

Lasswell's Model

He extended the scope of Aristotle's model of communication by laying emphasis on the channel which the speaker selected to bring about a change in the thinking process of the receiver. He laid stress on three factors - the speaker, the message, and the channel. This model as well talked of the one way direction of communication (Kaul, 2001).

Shannon Weaver Model

The earlier two concepts were integrated by them and emphasized the importance of encoding process prior to the transmission of the message. Model of communication process developed by Shannon and Weaver illustrated below suggests that the communication process is two phased. The first phase starts with the sender encoding the message and transmitting it to the receiver. The second phase commences with the decoding of the message with receiver's own frame of reference, encoding it and formulating it in the form of a response. Ultimately, this message reaches the original speaker and he decodes it based on his own frame of reference, resulting in the completion of the loop of communication. It was a step ahead of the existing models as it recognized the importance of existence of noise and its potential for distortion of communication. It further highlighted the significance of feedback for the completion of the communication cycle.

1. Chairman, DDE&EL, and Professor of HR and Business Communication, Institute of Management Technology, Hapur Road, Ghaziabad, U.P.

2. Faculty Member, HR and Business Communication, Institute of Management Technology, Hapur Road,

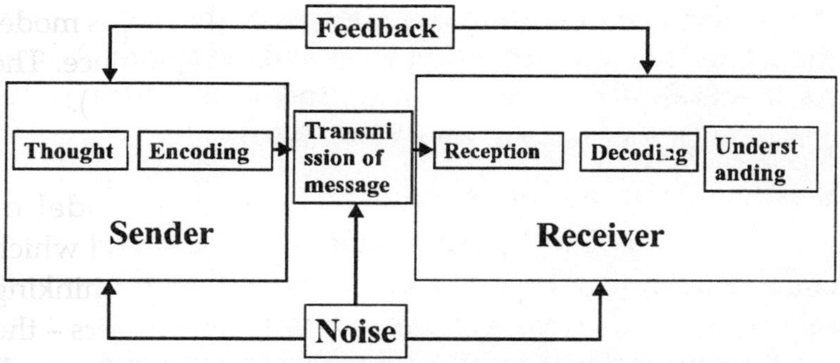

Illustration 1 : Communication Process Model, *Shannon Weaver*

Ghaziabad, U.P.

Schramm's Model

The best known model which has so far been proposed is of Wilbur Schramm in 1955. He proposed three models. Each one was an improvement of the existing one. The third model suggested by Schramm was a ground-breaking effort. It proposed for the first time the importance of response from the receiver. Together with the encoding of the message and transmission of the same through a proper channel, it necessitated that the receiver after decoding the message transmitted the response to the sender. The scope was now extended to encompass within it both the sender as well as the receiver together with the important component of the message and the feedback.The field of experience presented in the model connotes the frame of reference of individual within which he formulates his ideas of receiving the message. The various components in his model were: the source, encoding process, signal, decoding process, and destination (Kaul, 2001).

Katz-Lazarsfel's Model

They proposed a model which was more suitable for mass communication. According to them, the sender encoded the message and transmitted information through mass media to an opinion leader who finally relayed it to the public. The important components of this model were the sender, the receiver, the message and the opinion leader. As it was directed towards mass media the direction of communication was one way (Kaul, 2001).

Westley-Maclean's Model

The focus laid by the authors was on interpersonal communication. Their model suggests that the sender selectively encodes the message to be transmitted. It further suggests the receiver on decoding the message would again encode the message as a process of information transmission to either the original sender or to individuals in a modified form. They placed importance to the sender, the receiver, and feedback.

Berlo's Model

Berlo was the first to identify the role of perception in reception of the message. He pointed out that the sender would encode the message based on his skill and experience. Then the receiver receives it based on his understanding of words and their particular context. He further suggested a variance in the intended and the perceived message could create miscommunication. The direction of the model was one way. However, the important components were the source, the receiver, the meaning, and the process (Kaul, 2001).

Newcomb's Model

The flow of communication identified by him was triangular, wherein he laid stress on reaction of the people to each other and things discussed. He brought the significance of harmony and consistency in communication. The important contributors were the receiver and the meaning of associated words (Kaul, 2001).

Dance's Model

Dance recognized that a single piece of communication

does not occur in isolation rather it is rooted in the previous or prior communication experiences of the receiver. He pointed out that the encoding and decoding processes were dependent upon the history of communiqué. He even emphasized the importance of time taken in encoding and decoding. In fact, his model followed a helical-spiral path (Kaul, 2001).

Watlawwickz-Beavin-Jackobson's Model

According to them the communication was based on the behaviour of the interactants. The exchange message was largely dependent on the relationship between individuals and varied from one individual to another. They introduced a new element of miscommunication together with the receiver, meaning and process in explaining the outcome of communication. They were in all probability, the first to propose that the communication was a two way process (Kaul, 2001).

Rogers-Kincaid's Model

Rogers and Kincaid identified that the individuals need to be linked to one another through networks created and information shared. The major components of their work were social networks, information and time. The direction observed by this type of communication was spiral (Kaul, 2001).

The suggested model

Drawing from the essence of diverse propositions of communication models presented above, we intend to suggest a communication model which highlights the importance of the key factor in a communication process-feedback. The model isolates 13 elements during the process of communication impacting the quality and effectiveness of the receipt of the message by intended receiver. The model recognizes not only the role of perception in reception of the message but also stresses that the interpretation of the message is contingent on the previous history and behavior of the interactants. The model is presented diagrammatically below for superior understanding.

COMMUNICATION PROCESS MODEL-BAJAJ

The 13 elements/components are detailed below:

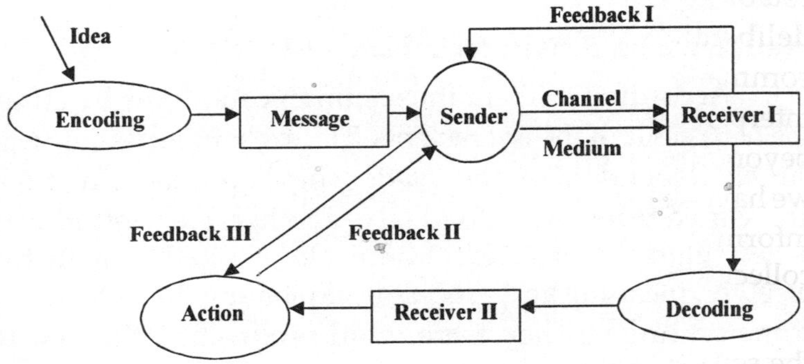

Illustration 2

1. Idea : An idea can acquire many forms and faces. It can be any fact, opinion, information or emotion that arises in the mind of the sender. The sender thinks of an idea to be communicated.

2. Encoding : Once an idea has occurred to the communicator it is encoded in a language understood by the sender. The sender also takes care that it is encoded in a language that is known to the receivers. The language chosen can be verbal or non-verbal. The encoding process is critical because it is contingent upon the skill and level of intelligence of the sender.

3. Message : Once the encoding process is complete, the idea takes the shape of a message. The idea is a raw material which is exposed to the process of encoding. The final product is the message tempered by the elements like the understanding of words, level of skill and intelligence of the sender.

4. Sender : The generator of the idea. The idea acquires its finer features and dimensions and takes the shape of a message. This message is the end result of the sender's contemplation process.

5. Channel : Channel can be formal or informal or even a mix of the two. Formal channel is one that follows the established network in the organization. This network is deliberately created and normally follows the chain of command. The informal channel is the result of social interpersonal relationships amid people. It normally extends beyond the boundaries of the formal channel. The mix that we have suggested above implies the dissemination of formal information in the guise of informal information in order to collect the reactions of the recipients.

6. Medium : Before the message travels to the receiver, the sender is required to select the medium through which the message would flow. Medium can be written, telephonic, or face to face meeting. The choice of medium selected by the sender is subject to many factors and considerations - Urgency of feedback, requirement for maintenance of legal record, complexity of information, demonstration and observation of facts and feelings.

7. Receiver I : The first person to receive the message is the receiver I. The person may be the secretary/assistant/ colleague in a business environment. Receiver I obtains the message directly from the sender through the sender's choice of selected medium and channel. The receiver then formulates his own understanding of the message based on his own frame of mind.

8. Decoding : Decoding is the process of conversion of the message as received from the sender in language understood by the receiver I. The receiver decodes the message received flavored with his own perception, understanding of words, level of skill and intelligence. The decoding is done on the basis of verbal as well as non-verbal cues.

9. Receiver II : The second recipient receives the message from the first one. For example, the first one can be the secretary and the second recipient could be the next in command to the initial sender.

10. Action : The intention of any message is to generate action from the recipient. No action can also be a form of action taken. For example, a subordinate waiting for response from the superior regarding a report submitted for revision of the accounting system gets the message that he should wait for the moment.

11. Feedback I : The first receiver on receipt of the message and post-decoding would give the feedback to the sender either about his understanding of the message, may seek more information from the sender or inform that the message has been forwarded to the desired person/recipient.

12. Feedback II : Desired action is accomplished by the second recipient and the information is forwarded to the sender. This is the feedback II. The feedback can be in the form of a report, oral or written.

13. Feedback III : The sender is updated on the latest information through feedback II. The sender may require a clarification about the information received or may extend words of praise or even reprimand as suitable. This is the third level feedback obtained. It is represented in the illustration II as feedback III.

Thus, a cycle of flow of communication is completed. Here it is essential to note the importance of the feedback received and specified. Without this feedback at each stage there is likely to be distortion of the message ultimately leading to miscommunication and soured relations. Therefore, the model lays stress on the feedback mechanisms to be established and their significance emphasized in organizations to ensure smooth and efficient flow of information.

Having developed a brief on the complete communication model, it is also necessary at this stage to look at the appropriate implementation methodology of teaching business communication.

In this regard, the recommendation of the new course outlines and the number of classroom teaching hours and credits that should be devoted to this are given as annexure I and annexure II. One's ability to communicate effectively increases productivity, both one's own and the organizations. One can shape the impressions we and the company make on colleagues, employees, supervisors, investors, and customers in addition to perceiving and responding to needs of these stakeholders. Without effective communication, people misunderstand each other. Ideas misfire or fail to get attention, and people and companies flounder. In fact, studies reveal that on an average, 14 per cent of each 40-hour work week is wasted because of poor communication between staff and management (Bovee, Thill, and Schatzman, 2003). Annexure I is the suggested curriculum for oral communication skills. The course starts with the basic orientation on essentials of communication in general.

For some, one of the easiest things in the world is to stand in front of a group of people and to talk. Others may tremble and rush for cover at the sight of an audience. Why this difference? Assuming that both speakers are familiar with the subject matter, we find that some excel in the art of making presentations while others run in the opposite direction. The difference lies in the attitude towards making presentations. Therefore, for a business manager it is essential to master the art of presentation. It is suggested that adequate time is devoted to preparing students to become smart, effective and fearless presenters. In fact, if students' presentations are video recorded and replayed, the effect is intriguing. They are immediately charged up to advance their presentations skills. Subsequent, similar recording and replays bring out effortlessly the extent of progress that has taken place. By the time they make the third presentation which need not be recorded, considerable perfection is achieved and each student is able to develop his/her own personal unique style.

Most literature on business communication detail the different aspects and technicalities of conducting meetings but remain silent about conferences. In fact with the global economies, it has become common for organizations to conduct small or large conferences. We suggest the inclusion of this in the curriculum for oral communication. A detailed content list of steps in conducting a conference/meeting is included as annexure III.

Guests from high context culture, such as Japan, rely less on verbal communication and more on circumstances and non-verbal actions to communicate their messages. So rather than complaint directly to the employees, Japanese guests expect employees to anticipate their needs. Other behavioral differences are more overt. For example, when a hotel receptionist pulls out a chair for a Japanese woman, the woman's husband will typically sit down first, thinking that the receptionist has pulled it out for him. Gestures are another big difference. In fact, Japanese guests find some western forms of non-verbal communication offensive, including leaning on the wall, using an index finger to summon someone, and moving things with ones' feet. So the employees at Sheraton Hotels, Hawaii, are instructed to avoid these offensive behaviors and communicate in ways that guests are accustomed to, as a part of sensitivity training program (Bovee, Thill, and Schatzman, 2003). Now this is not unique to the hospitality industry alone. In fact, it has become an inevitable reality for all organizations as a result of three phenomenons – global market place, multi-cultural work force and business process outsourcing. In global marketplace, national borders have disappeared, for most part, as more and more markets open to worldwide competition and as business look for new growth opportunities for their goods and services. Today's workforce is increasingly made up of people who differ in race, gender, age, culture, family structure, religion, and educational background. Such cultural diversity is the second trend contributing to the importance of intercultural communication. It affects how business messages are conceived, planned, sent, received, and interpreted in the workplace. The latest trend, particularly in India, is the fast growth of the business process outsourcing industry, heralding the need for healthier understanding of cross cultural communication.

Business etiquette is the practice of polite and appropriate behavior in the business setting. Business etiquette differs in many ways from social etiquette. The manager who enumerates all his or her accomplishments to the superior during a performance appraisal is simply being savvy; the manager who does so during a social engagement is being boorish. You must be sensitive to what is appropriate under any given circumstances (Ober, 2005).

Good manners translate into good business; they convey a strong positive message about you as a person. As Mark Twain once observed about etiquette, "always do right, you will please some people and astonish the rest". The students of business management need to be well versed in the knack of business etiquette. They should be able to cruise through any business circumstance with ease and dexterity. Both surgeons and tailors work with needles, threads and scissors; yet the level of finesse, dexterity, expertise and proficiency required by them is remarkably different.

Mental block – this is not a word alien to anyone who as ever written a letter, report, message, memo or e-mail. The written word is more potent than the strengths of the toughest men put together. Well-turned but appropriate phrases and words can buoy up communication that is otherwise likely to sink into the oblivion of files and waste paper baskets. No one can escape writing. Improved and sophisticated telephonic, mobile, and satellite communication had replaced the traditional and staid letters at a point in time. On the other hand, with the popularity of e-mail, the importance of the written word has been regained. Therefore, it is essential that students of professional courses are exposed to the elements, techniques and intricacies of written communication. Annexure II presents the curriculum for written communication. E-mail's beauty, power, and easy accessibility have naturally attracted millions of users all over the world. Their tribe, over 300 million in first quarter of 2001, is growing incredibly fast (Monipally, 2001). In the developed world, more than two-thirds of all companies now use e-mail for regular communication. It is estimated that at Microsoft Corporation alone there are more than 4 million internal and external e-mail messages passing through their system every single day (Monipally, 2001). E-mail is also being used for internal communication. Firms have intranet or private networks. Quite frequently memos are being replaced with e-mails. E-mail is like a sharp butcher's knife. It cuts effortlessly. But only a fool will try and use it for heart surgery (Monipally, 2001). Thus, it is essential that e-mails are awarded equal place of honor with letters. Therefore, we strongly recommend the inclusion of e-mails: safety, presenting mail, e-mail etiquette, and managing the mailbox in the course curriculum. Similarly, we are inundated with information overload. The art of reading can be of vital help here. Thus, the curriculum on written communication includes both tips to improve reading habit, speed of reading and the e-mail commonsense and etiquette-'netiquette' as it is usually called.

Further, we strongly recommend that the two courses

– written and oral communication, should be taught as separate subjects with full credits. It is also recommended that the strength of a batch for oral communication should be not more than 25 students. A class of 60 students can be divided into three batches of 20 students each. This is important to ensure tangible improvement in communication skills of the students. Personalized attention and focus is not possible if the course is to be taught to 60 students with the limitation of 30 sessions of 60 minutes each. In fact, here we would like to quote from Ludlow and Paton, "Developing communication skills is like learning to play contract bridge. You need to learn the rules and the conventions. You also need a partner to practice with and you need to learn how well you are doing, so that you can improve on your areas of weakness in bidding or playing. And it is only with practice and feedback that you will develop into a good bridge player or an effective communicator. So the emphasis must be on empirical learning – learning by doing – and on receiving feedback."

SECTION II : DELIVERY MECHANISM WITH A DIFFERENCE

The traditional manner of teaching is inadequate for the dynamic and ever evolving course on business communication. The primary reason being that the fast paced changes in technology are followed closely by changes in the way people communicate and understand each other. Unlike other management courses business communication is purely practical in nature and is needed at all times during the waking hours. It needs to be strategic in the sense of a healthy, long term relationship between the communicator and the communicatee. The acquired knowledge and expertise losses its cutting edge in case it fails to be communicated to the recipient. The desired impact of any communique is lost if not cradled by appropriate communication skills. Thus, we suggest the following:

Theory

No one can communicate effectively if he or she cannot communicate correctly. It is imperative that the students are exposed to the overall framework of business communication. The theory is essentially the foundation on which the building is constructed. Without adequate exposure to theoretical inputs, the communication skills developed would lack solid grounding. It is an unfortunate fact of life that many contemporary students today have not had the advantage of the nuts-and-bolt grammar and mechanics that their instructors took for granted in their own prior education. Therefore, the course must throw some spotlight on common grammatical errors and understanding of words. For example, it is not uncommon for students to confuse between aspect, accept, and expect similarly between assess and access.

Discussion – Interactive Participation

Students learn to communicate by communicating – not by just reading about communicating. The instructor may draw on students to promote class-room discussion. Discussions and interactive participation prompt students to stretch their learning beyond the conceptual framework. Instructors can use this opportunity to promote classroom discussion on issues that have no easy answers. The sessions become more inspiring and stimulating leaving the brain cells tingling with flow of new knowledge and ideas.

Audio - Visual Aids

Interactive sessions come alive and become charged with students' expressive responses when the concepts are supported with audio-visual clips from real business world situations. For example, communication barriers become fascinating and acquire a new facet when taught through the help of a clipping showcasing a mis-communication in an organization. The impact and learning generated with the help of these aids is ingrained and the students rarely forget it. The dry subject like business communication suddenly becomes engrossing to the contemporary business acumen. Similarly, session on body language can be supported through clipping from silent, classic or latest movies to bring home the connotation, consequences, and flavor of body language in the communication process.

Case Study Method

Brain is more easily stimulated by words on paper than one's minds' eye. Case study method is a tool for demonstrating the role of communication in the real business world. Exercises and cases emphasize on providing practical assignments that students will most often face at work – both domestic and international. They reinforce basic concepts by examining critical issues that face business communicators in today's workplace. Students gain insight into how to identify areas of vulnerability, how to steer clear of perils, and when to seek advice.

Documents for Analysis

The faculty should provide wide selection of documents that students can critique and revise. Documents can include letters, memos, e-mail messages, letter of application, résumé, or an invitation. Documents can be utilized including poor and improved examples, to illustrate common errors and effective techniques for correcting them. Hands-on experience in analyzing and improving sample documents will help students revise their own business messages. They provide useful guidelines for writing, without limiting creativity.

Presentations

Delivering presentations is an inherent part of work environment. Frequently managers are called upon to make presentations. It is imperative that students understand the benefits and disadvantages of giving presentations. They are aware of their own individual strengths and weaknesses in presenting, and of how they can use their own style to best advantage. They should be able to identify and tackle the effect of "nerves" on their ability to present. Students should be aware of issues involved in working with an audience. They should be able to select and use visual aids appropriately. Developing presentation skills - prepared as well as impromptu is an inherent component of the course on business communication.

Practical Scenario-Practice

Practical pointers and confidence building guidelines help students improve their writing and speaking skills. Practical guidelines enable students strengthen their career skills by exploring diverse ordinary and extra ordinary topics. Specific techniques offer students guidance for using technological applications to improve business communication. The technique emphasizes the skill and competencies necessary for students to induce transition from business school to the workplace. Role plays prompt the students to stretch their learning beyond conceptual limits.

Project Work with the Industry

To help students organize their thinking when they do a communication project, take decisions as they write and check their own work. Industry interaction provides the on the job essence to the students. It allows them to reinforce the learning with richer contextual clues to solve communication problems. Students become intimately familiar with the managers and the company and must select what is relevant from a mass of data, thereby learning to handle information overload. This provides an occasion for work team communication and critical thinking skills.

SECTION III : FEEDBACK AND EVALUATION SYSTEM PEDAGOGY TO INCLUDE BOTH STUDENTS AND INDUSTRY

The need to communicate is universal and transcends every man-made classification based on language, place, or culture (Ober, 2005). A course on business communication prepares students for the accelerated pace of business communication by bridging the road from concept to practice. Students require no convincing about the need for competent communication skills. By the time they enter the business communication class, students know sufficiently about business environment to appreciate the critical role communication plays in the contemporary organization.

The onset of the twenty first century has heralded fast paced changes in technology, business models and environment translating into new forms, types and ways of communication. Today, if there is one business buzzword, it has to be "technology" and with good reason. Every aspect of contemporary business communication – from determining what information to communicate to processing the information and sharing it depends on technology. A course in business communication needs to self-evaluate and reinvent itself in order to respond to these changes. This requires a self updating mechanism needs to be developed. For this we suggest the following:

Feedback from Students

Daily feedback after the end of the session

A continuous feedback methodology allows the instructor to be sensitive to the pulse of the students. Daily feedback is primarily oral in nature. In fact, the instructor can ascertain the students' response through their expressions and mannerisms during the session itself.

Weekly feedback

While a daily feedback takes the immediate pulse, a weekly feedback would play the role of evaluating things on supplementary data and forming a trend analysis, thereby ensuring that knee-jerk decisions are not taken. The mechanism enables the instructor to modify and lay stress on those aspects of the course as maybe the unique requirement of each batch. In fact, our colleague fraternity will agree that each batch of students is a repository of a different set of skills, competency and fluency. The weekly feedback may be oral as well as written or through online feedback system. It has been our experience that students actively participate in offering their views, apprehensions, and concerns.

Feedback at the end of the course

Feedback at the end of the course can be taken from the students in order to ascertain the efficacy of the subject taught as per the annexure IV. This enables the instructor to design far superior courseware for the next batches to come. The learners log is for the students' benefit, to enable them to chart their progress throughout the term. It is revisited in class briefly at the beginning of each session and in more detail halfway through the term and finally, at the end of the term to evaluate the course. The learners log enables the students to log the three things they learnt, skills they developed, and some things they need to work on at the end of each session. This is step by step dossier for their as well as teachers reference.

Self Evaluation by Faculty

Self evaluation by faculty is incessant process monitoring the feedback constantly. Together with the students and the learners log the instructor can assess for themselves the effectiveness of the course taught.

Feedback and Evaluation from the Industry in General and From Alumni in Particular

No doubt the feedback from industry and alumni in particular is of utmost magnitude. They are in a position to share the ground realities, requirements, and potential for the future. Once they are extended an opportunity to give frank and pertinent feedback, worthwhile results can be obtained. It is a vital tool which can be utilized to blend the course with the effervescent business environment.

SECTION IV : COURSE CURRICULUM UPDATION MECHANISM - KAIZEN TEIAN

Kaizen Teian is a Japanese concept which revolutionalized the implementation of the suggestion scheme in industry which had become almost dormant. The concept basically considers that the person working on the job is the master of his job and the best person to suggest as well as implement the improvements in his area of work. Another important philosophy of Kaizen Teian is small continual improvements rather than any extraordinary improvement in a single big leap. Through this the concept recognizes that it is easier to progress through practical and small continual improvements which are not capital intensive.

Any activity losses its sheen and relevance to the contemporary issues unless it is continuously revised in the light of the dynamic environment. The business world is incessantly evolving and new structure and forms of operation are sprouting each day. The business communication course has to vigorously respond to these changes based on feedback and evaluation the course curriculum to be updated every year involving faculty, industry, alumni and students. We suggest the application of concept of Kaizen Teian to the course on business communication. Each, howsoever small, change is recognized and implemented. These small changes would ultimately result in the final product turning out to be more industry responsive, relevant, effective and practical.

CONCLUSION

There is a growing recognition that effective business communication is necessary for making an impact on the interpersonal relationships. Good communication skills have always been important in the workplace. They are even more vital today, when the changing workplace has brought these communication challenges: advances in technology, globalization, an increasing culturally diverse workforce, and the adoption of team-based organizational structures. Fed by global competition and global opportunities, contemporary organizations are making extensive use of project management, continuous process improvement, and work teams to encourage their employees to work and communicate collaboratively to solve complex workplace problems. Thus, competent communicators need to develop high level interpersonal skills for working in small groups as well as for writing and presenting collaboratively.

Emerging areas in communication are issues relating to customer-centric communication, employment related communication and ethical and cross cultural communication, some specific topics that can be explored further are those relating to gender roles in communication and leadership communication. In an increasing age of customer orientation, communication syllabi, as existing in various B-Schools needs to move beyond internal perspective to include external perspective also (Mehra, 2005).

In this paper we have developed a communication process model which emphasizes the role of feedback at different stages. The paper also suggests a course curriculum for oral and written communication. We further suggest that the two should be taught separately as full credit papers. The paper outlines in detail a delivery mechanism with a difference. It suggests use of audio-visual aids to make the classes interactive and liven up the classes and make them more effective. The paper further considers a feedback and evaluation system pedagogy to include both students and industry such that a continuous evaluation process is possible to make the subject responsive to the dynamic business environment (Kaizen Teian).

REFERENCES

Bovee, C. L. and Thill, J. V. and Schatzman, B. E. (2003) Business Communication Today, Pearson Education.

Kaul, Asha. (2001), Business Communication, Prentice Hall of India.

Kaul, Asha. (2001), Effective Business Communication, Prentice Hall of India.

Ludlow, Ron and Panton, Fergus (2002), The Essence of Effective Communication, Adrian Buckley (Ed), Prentice Hall of India

Mehra, Payal. (2005), Managers' Perception of Importance of Business Communication for Effective Job Performance: An Empirical Evaluation, The Icfaian Journal of Management Research, September.

Monipally, Mutthukutty. M., (2001), Business Communication Strategies, Tata McGraw-Hill Publishing Company Limited.

Ober, Scot., (2005), Contemporary Business Communication, Biztantra, fifth edition, Indian adaptation.

Robinson, David, (2003), Effective Communication and Business Skills, Biztantra.

Taylor, Shirley. (2002), Communication for Business, Pearson Education Asia.

ANNEXURE I : ORAL COMMUNICATION

S.No.		Topic	Indicative Hours
1.		Communication in General	3
	a.	What is Communication?	
	b.	Role Of Communication In Business Organizations and Day Today Life	
	c.	Communication Process Model and its Characteristics	
	d.	Various Types of Communication	
	e.	Communication Barriers and How To Overcome Them	
	f.	Types And Channels Of Communication	
	g.	Perception And Reality	
2.		Effective Listening Skills	2
	a.	Effective Listening – Difference Between Hearing and Listening	
	b.	Inefficiency Of Listening – Improving Your Listening Ability	
	c.	Class Discussion – Role Of Effective Listening Towards Organizational Excellence.	
	d.	Listening Exercises	
3.		Business Presentations	5
	a.	Impromptu Presentations	
	b.	Prepared Presentations	
	c.	Presentation Techniques	
	d.	Determination Of Personal Aspects – Advance Analysis	
	e.	Appearance And Body Actions	
	f.	Use Of Voice And Visual Aids	
		Individual Presentations by Students, their Evaluation and Feedback*	

4.	Conducting Meetings		6
	a.	Techniques Of Conducting Meetings	
		* Agenda	
		* Quorum	
		* Minutes of Meeting	
		* Chairpersons Role And Language	
		* Group Think and Group Shift	
	b.	Class Discussion on Problems of Meetings And Contributing to A Productive Meeting	
5.	Steps in Conducting Conferences/ Meetings		3
	a.	Pre-conference/meeting	
	b.	During conference/meeting	
	c.	Post conference address and vote of thanks	
6.	Group Discussion		3
	a.	Pedagogy To Conduct Group Discussion	
	b.	Class Discussion On "The Importance Of Listening And Nonverbal Messages In Interpersonal Communication"	
	c.	Body Language	
7.	Negotiations		2
	a.	What Is Negotiation?	
	b.	Negotiation Process – Conflict	
	c.	Effective Negotiation Techniques And Skills	
	d.	Negotiation, Mediation, & Arbitration Techniques	
	e.	Soft Skills	
8.	Business Etiquette		3
	a.	Meeting and Greeting	

	b.	Dining	
	c.	Giving Gifts	
	d.	Dressing Appropriately	
9.	Intercultural Communication		3
	a.	Inter, Intra, Cross Cultural Communication.	
	b.	Culture Subculture Ethnocentrism	
	c.	Cultural Context	
	d.	Legal And Ethical Behavior	
	e.	Social Behavior Differences	
	f.	Nonverbal Communication	
	g.	Overcoming Ethnocentrism	
	h.	Doing Business Abroad	
	i.	ESL Communication Barriers	
	j.	Foreign Language Barriers	
	k.	HCM, PCM, TCM	
	l.	Effective Expatriate Policy	
	m.	Effective Repatriate Policy	
	Total		**30**

ANNEXURE II : WRITTEN COMMUNICATION

S.No.	*Topic*		*Indicative Hours*
1.	**Grammar Problem**		**3**
	a.	Quality Aspects Of Communication	
	b.	Fundamentals Of Grammar And Usage	
	c.	How It Affects Effective Written Communication?	
2.	**Essay And Précis Writing**		**2**
	a.	Class Discussion - Live Examples From The Industry	
3.	**Principles Of Clear Business Writing And Effective Communications Model – Taking Down Notes In Seminars/Lectures/From Reference Material**		**1**
4.	**Effective Reading:**		**4**
	a.	Ingredients And Pedagogy Of Effective Reading	
		i. How to improve reading habit?	
		ii. How to improve speed of reading?	
	b.	To Bring Home By Video Recording And Replay	
5.	**Preparation Of Curriculum–Vitae**		**3**
	a.	Techniques	
	b.	Variety	
	c.	Effect	
6.	**Written Presentation of Technical Material – Preparation and Presentation Techniques Etc.**		**6**
7.	**Basic Official Correspondence**		**6**
	a.	Business Letters and Memo Writing Including Social Correspondence.	
		i. Compulsory elements/optional elements	
		ii. Layout and form	

		iii.	Types of letters - letter of recommendation, letter of introduction, letter of congratulation, informal and formal invitation, letter of condolence, notice	
		iv.	E-mail - safety, presenting mail, e-mail etiquette, managing the mail box	
		v.	Persuasive writing	
		vi.	Class exercise on letter writing	
	c.	Reports		
		i.	Structure	
		ii.	What is a formal report?	
		iii.	Preparatory steps	
		iv.	Types	
		v.	Letter and memo reporting	
		vi.	Discussion On Formats And Class Assignment On Physical Presentation Of Reports	
8.	**Case Analysis Methodology**			**3**
	a.	What is Case Study?		
	b.	Why Case Study?		
	c.	SWOT Analysis and Case Study Technique		
	d.	Discussion Of A Case Study		
9.	**Technology, Methodology For Effective Communication**			**2**
	a.	Early Development Of Communication Technology		
	b.	Advent Of Electronic And Other Technology		
	c.	Teleconferences		
	d.	Class Discussion - A New Look To The Future		
	Total			**30**

ANNEXURE III : STEPS IN CONDUCTING CONFERENCES/MEETINGS

1. Pre Conference/Meeting
   a. Preparation of tentative agenda and issue of circular notices/letters etc.
   b. Formalization of agenda, venue, date, time and other formalities
   c. Reception and documentations
   d. Transportation to the venue
   e. Seating plan and layout.
2. During Conference/Meeting
   a. Opening/address by the chair
   b. Conduct of the conference/meeting
   c. Writing minutes
   d. Closing address and vote of thanks.
3. Post Conference/Meeting
   a. Seeing off participants
   b. Issue of minutes of Conference/Meeting
   c. Follow up action and feedback.

ANNEXURE IV : BUSINESS COMMUNICATION LEARNER LOG

The following log is for your benefit, to enable you to chart your progress throughout the term. It will be revisited in class briefly at the beginning of each session and in more detail half way through the term and finally, at the end of the term to help evaluate the course.

SESSION 1 : SESSION SUMMARY

3 Things I Learnt

Skills I Developed

Something I Need To Work On

SESSION 2 : SESSION SUMMARY

3 Things I Learnt

Skills I Developed

Something I Need To Work On

SESSION 3 : SESSION SUMMARY

3 Things I Learnt

Skills I Developed

Something I Need To Work On

5

Leadership Communication: Decoding the Mystique

*Neerja Pande**

ABSTRACT

Those powerful and mysterious creatures we call 'leaders' have always fascinated the human imagination. Mahatma Gandhi, Nelson Mandela, Jack Welch, Mother Teresa, Lee Iacocca, Bill Gates, Narayana Murthy, Rudolph Giuliani – how we wish to know their minds a little better. Last few decades have seen an unprecedented interest in leadership issues. What is the secret of these leaders charisma? We wonder. Why do we get mesmerized by their talk and follow them like charmed children of Hamyln? What are those internal forces and motivations, which drive them? The present paper would attempt to break the DNA of a leader, with a focus on simplifying the complexities of leadership communication. The belief is that this might hasten the prospects of many of us to transform from a manager to a leader.

KEYWORDS : Effective Communication, Leadership Communication Logos, Pathos, Ethos, Empathic Listening.

"In describing today's accelerating changes, the media fires blips of unrelated information at us. Experts bury us under mountains of narrowly specialized monographs.

---

* Associate Professor and Chairperson Communication Area, Indian Institute of Management, Lucknow.

Popular forecasters present list of unrelated trends, without any model to show us their interconnections or the forces likely to reverse them. As a result, change itself comes to be seen as anarchic, even lunatic."

The above statement by Alvin Toffler sums up the importance of communication, especially in today's world. This in effect, doesn't mean that communication was not important earlier or it was less important than it is now. Communication was, is and will always remain an important and integral part of human life. But the world now has become so closely knitted and full of information that the utmost use of effective communication has become that much more important. The leader who works most effectively is the one who is able to distinguish and extract the useful and relevant information from the heap of information because "effective leadership is still largely a matter of communication."

Those powerful and mysterious creatures we call 'leaders' have always fascinated the human imagination. Mahatma Gandhi, Nelson Mandela, General Macarthur, Sir Winston Churchill, Jack Welch, Mother Teresa, Lee Iacocca, Bill Gates, Narayana Murthy, Rudolph Giuliani, — how we wish to know their minds a little better. Warren Bennis writes that whether or not leadership is well understood, its impact on the bottom line is dramatic, according to a study by Andersen Consulting's Institute for Strategic Change, the stock price of companies perceived as being well led grew 900 percent over a 10-year period, compared to just 74 percent growth in companies perceived to lack good leadership. And Fortune, in its 1998 round up of America's most admired companies, identifies the common denominator of exemplary organizations. "The truth is that no one factor makes a company admirable" wrote Thomas Stewart, "but if you were forced to pick the one that makes the most difference, you'd pick leadership". In Warren Buffet's phrase, "People are voting for the artist and not the painting".

Last few decades have seen an unprecedented interest in leadership issues. What is the secret of these leaders' charisma? We wonder. Why do we get mesmerized by their talk and follow them like charmed children of Hamyln? What are those internal forces and motivations which drive them? Like the poet in Robert Bridges' *Nightingales,* we wonder what kind of a world these leaders inhabit and aspire to visit that world to improve our own prospects as leaders?

"Beautiful must be the mountains where ye come,
And bright in the fruitful valleys the streams,
Wherefrom
Ye learn your song;
Where are those starry woods?
O might I wander there,"

A review of the scholarly studies on leadership shows that there is a wide variety of different theoretical approaches to explain the complexity of the leadership process (e.g., Bass, 1990; Bryman, 1992; Gardener, 1990; Hickman, 1998; Rost, 1991). Some researchers conceptualize leadership as a trait, or as behavior, while others view leadership from a political perspective, or from a humanistic viewpoint collectively, the research findings on leadership from all of these areas provide a picture of a process that is far more sophisticated and complex than the often simplistic view presented.

The present paper would attempt to break the DNA of a leader, with a focus on simplifying the complexities of leadership communication even further and deconstructing the mystique. The belief is that this might hasten the prospects of many of us to metamorphoses from a manager to a leader.

What Is Leadership Communication?

Leadership is a complex process by which, a person influences others and directs the organization in a way that makes it more cohesive and coherent. A person carries out this process by applying her leadership attributes i.e. beliefs, values, ethics, character, knowledge, soft skills. According to Peter Drucker, "Leadership is the lifting of man's vision to higher sights, the raising of means performance to higher standards, the building of mans personality beyond the normal limitations".

Effective communication provides the very lifeblood leaders need to move forward, to focus organizations on worthy goals, and to motivate action. Without effective communication, leaders stumble and fail. Leadership and effective communication are more than directly correlated, they are inseparable. The big question is whether a man is boom with this influencing capability or he can acquire it. And the big answer is that that like anything else, the ability to communicate clearly and persuasively is a skill that can be learned and acquired.

As Mintzberg notes, "Verbal and written contacts are the managers' (leaders) work". He goes on, "Managers (leaders) must be able to communicate easily and efficiently, and they must share a vision of the direction in which they wish to take their organization. If they cannot agree with reasonable precision on these "plans", then they will pull in different directions and the team (organization) will break down."

A leader then is a person who becomes differentiated from other members in leans of influence he exerts upon the goal-setting and goal-achievement activities of the organization.

Some are boom great some have greatness thrust on them and some achieve greatness. Gone are the days of any other type of leader except the third. No one is marked for subjection or command from the hour of their birth in the context of present day organization. To be a leader in today's context you have to achieve it and achievement can come only through preparation.

Let us look at Leadership Communication from the basic structure of the applications of the three fundamental rules of persuasion: logos, pathos and ethos and attempt to decode the mystique of Leadership Communication.

Aristotle's -*The Art of Rhetoric*

Aristotle thought that a public speaker should possess good character, have common sense, and be concerned for the well being of the audience. Quintillion, a Roman teacher of public speaking, also felt that an effective speaker should be a person of good character. Quintillion's advice was that a speaker should be a "good man speaking well."

D. H. Lawrence might have said it in some other context "Trust the tale and not the artist". Will Durant also might have urged in *The Story of Philosophy*, "and do not mind whether the teachers of philosophy are good or bad, but think only of Philosophy herself". But this does not hold true for the leaders of today. 'Messenger is the message.' We believe the message only if we believe the messenger, thus, it becomes imperative for leaders to first and foremost be authentic and credible people if they want their message to hold any water with their audience.

Aristotle spoke directly and often to this issue in the first, and still the best, general study of communication, his *Rhetoric*. The books most important contribution was identifying the three elements of persuasion common to any argument. He defined three essential qualities of successful communication: *logos* (the logic of the argument), *pathos* (the emotional impact of the argument) and *ethos* (the values represented or expressed by the speaker). These elements allow us to make sense of any argument, no matter who makes it. *The Art of Rhetoric* contains several lengthy chapters on human character and emotions: "the orator... must be both a logician and a psychologist. Rhetoric can then be seen as precisely a mixture of these two disciplines."

In a modernE restatement of these basics, the authors of *The Challenge of Organizational Change* write, "Effective communication addresses both cognitive needs (for facts, data, 'hard' information, analysis) and emotional needs (for reassurance, comfort, sympathy, feeling of connection). And it reinforces the values and invokes the symbols that keep the organization together."

Who are You-Ethos

Leadership communication depends on the ability to project a positive image, or more specifically, a positive ethos, inside an organization and outside. The word "image" is often associated with illusion or superficiality. It embodies what an audience thinks of you initially based on mostly superficial perceptions. Ethos refers to qualities of greater depth and substance. It ties more directly to your character, which your audience judges according to the culture in which you are communicating.

"It's no exaggeration to say that a strong positive self-image is the best possible preparation for leadership in life." The Greek philosopher, sitting in the garden, at the dead of night, brooding on the big questions of life and existence when asked by the guard on duty "who are you" had the luxury of giving the reply 'Had I known that' as an answer and getting away with it but the leaders of today do not have that luxury. *Gnothi seauton* 'Know thyself holds truer for them than anybody else".

Leaders not only have to know who they are but they also have to incessantly work towards removing any follies and foibles present in their character for their communication in future is going to be believed only if their character is worthy. While it is crucial to master the tools of communication analysis and the technique of effective delivery, ultimately your success as a communicator will depend heavily on how you are perceived as a person. Here's the deal : learning to be a leader is virtually the same process as becoming an integrated and healthy person. Or as Shakespeare put it, "Learning is but an adjunct of our selves.". What that means is that when we talk about 'growing leaders', we're inevitably involved in personal stuff, personal transformation.

A positive ethos will take you a long way toward influencing your audiences with your intended message, whereas a negative ethos is one of the greatest barriers to effective communication. How you are perceived makes the difference in how well you are believed, how persuasive you are, and ultimately, how effectively you communicate. Successful leadership communication depends on projecting a positive ethos.

A final note on skillful rhetoric: none of it will work if the change leader doesn't personally embody the message. An attitude of "Do as I say, not as I do" will come across loud and clear, dooming any attempt to create change. Among the various commands, policies, practices, and suggestions that come from above subordinates select those most in keeping with their perception of their bosses' character, personal motivation, and style and give them priority. . . . if the immediate boss does not feel personally responsible for a given matter, the subordinates will not either.

In other words, you have to walk the talk. Otherwise, it's all just manipulation- the kind of verbal trickery that gives rhetoric a bad name. Good rhetoric is similar to the magic words of folklore: like *abracadabra* and *open sesame,* the words only work if you believe in them.

It is all in the words: Logos

'All leaders, believe it or not, are in the business of

words'. Once you have examined your position as the source of communicator, you have to focus on the message and decide how to frame the message in such a way that it is able to give you the anticipated positive response. You might have the most infallible character in the organization but that does not mean that you will become a great communicator or a great leader by the power of your character only.

"The man who can think but does not know how to express what he thinks is at the same level as he who cannot think." So opines Pericles, leader of Athens around 450 BC.

The ability to craft frames may well be the essence of persuasion and leadership. This essentially is *Logos* or the logic of the argument given by Aristotle in his *Rhetoric*. Logos, persuasion based on reason, logic, and "the facts", appeal to the rational mind; the realm of persuasion here is that of the syllogism, definitions, and logical fallacies. Logic is a formal system of rules for making inferences. When used rigorously, logic can make your arguments absolutely convincing. The use of a frame will vary depending on the persuader's specific agenda and forum. A frame could be the title of a speech a CEO hopes will rally the troops. The CEO establishes the big picture and the perceptual filter he wants the audience to employ while listening to the message. By entitling the speech "My Vision, You Gain". He establishes the frame by linking his corporate vision with employees personal needs.

When we frame a message, we achieve three interrelated goals. First, we select an evaluative theme or perspective believed to be the most credible, compelling, and appropriate to our intent. That perspective provides a filter through which we want the other party to assess our position and the supporting evidence. Second, we decide on the specific evidence that best supports that perspective. Finally, we create a structure for organizing mat evidence. Thus, the frame provides the perspective we want the other party to adopt, a rationale for the evidence we present, and the sequential pattern for presenting that evidence.

Consider this analogy, suppose you and a colleague wagered on who could complete the same jigsaw puzzle first. A third party buys two copies of the same 350-piece puzzle, dumping the contents of both boxes on a table in front of each of you. Your opponent has access to the box with a picture of the completed puzzle. You do not. Who will win? A frame is to a persuasive argument as the picture of a completed puzzle is to the jumbled pieces of the puzzle. Both show the "big picture" and provide implicit rules for putting the pieces together. Without the picture and without the frame, chaos prevails over coherence.

Logos essentially means command of the language. Have you chosen the right words? Have you built them into clear, coherent sentences? Does each paragraph convey a succinct unit of thought? Have you identified all the relevant data and constructed a convincing argument? Do you in short have the fundamental skills to be an effective communicator? This Aristotelian category includes many crucial qualities, such as a command of structure and style.

Structural explanations, when they are clear and widely understood, have considerable impact. An exceptional example of a leader providing such insight was Franklin Roosevelt, when he went on the radio on March 12, 1933, to explain the four day banking holiday. In a time of panic, Roosevelt calmly explained how the banking system worked, structurally. "Let me state the simple fact that when you deposit money in a bank the bank does not put the money in a safe deposit vault," he said. "It invests your money in many different forms of credit—bonds, mortgages etc. In other words, the bank puts your money to work to keep the wheels turning around..." He explained how banks were required to maintain reserves , but how these reserves were inadequate if there were widespread withdrawals and why closing the bank was necessary action, and began his reputation as a master of public communications.

Harvard Professor Howard Gardner says "Leadership involves the creation of powerful narratives..... that are much more than mission statements or messages. They are actual stories where there are goals and obstacles, where good and bad things can happen along the way, and where people involved feel part of an enterprise that's trying to end up in a better place. This once again demonstrates that felicity with words and power of invoking an image in the minds of the listeners goes a long way in establishing the leader as powerful motivator. It is essential that the leaders should have a vision, but it is also essential that the leader should be able to articulate this vision clearly and forcefully on all occasions.

The Emotional Wiring : Pathos

There are some who say, "To sell John Brown what John Brown buys, you have to see through John Browns eyes". Pathos means command of your own and the audiences' emotions. Emotions may seem out of place in a business setting, but in fact they play a major role in every interaction. Pathos also contains an idea of empathy-individuals and mass audience alike will be more prone to support someone who understands their point of view, even if they disagree. Most important, the ability to appeal to an audiences' sense of justice, fair play and human dignity matters as much in a business situation as in other communications, and it can sometimes override a call to narrow personal advantage.

Like a good psychologist, skillful rhetoricians listen closely before they make recommendations for change. As Jan Carlzon explained in an HBS lecture, he crafted his rhetorical strategy for turning around SAS only after "listening very carefully... to many different groups of people: managers, people on the front line, union people".

Good listening helps change managers get a reality check on the organization and tailor the change message accordingly to different groups. Also, listening can prevent a change initiative from being blindsided by resistance. Change managers must continuously take the temperature of the organization to understand what forms resistance may take. This is particularly important since, as one change veteran noted, managers almost always overestimate their understanding of their organization.

With top-down communication the norm, and barriers to bottom-up communication almost built in to organizations, skilful change initiators must sometimes resort to artificial means to "pump and pipe" information upward. Jack Welch's Work-Out program was bom out of this need for information. The program was devoted almost exclusively to airing the concerns of employees; with the help of outside facilitators, workers arrived at a list of proposals which they presented to their managers at the end of me three-day session. The managers then responded in one of the three ways: with immediate approval or disapproval, or by asking for more information and committing to a decision within a fixed period. This rhetorical principle is somewhat different from the others since, in Welch's words, it "means more listening than talking". But listening brings numerous benefits to managers, beyond minimizing surprise attacks; in fact, it seems that simply allowing people to air their concerns builds trust and defuses resistance.

According to Stephen R. Covey, when another person speaks, we are usually listening at one of the four levels. First level is when we may be ignoring another person and not listening at all. Then we may also pretend and show as if we are listening. We may practice selective listening, i.e. hearing only parts of the conversation. Or we may even practice attentive listening. Paying attention and focusing energy on the words that are being said. But very few of us ever practice the fifth level, the highest form of listening which Stephen Covey calls 'empathic listening'.

Empathic listening involves much more than just registering, reflecting or even understanding the words that are said. Communication experts estimate that only about ten percent of our communication is represented by the words we say. Another 30 per cent is represented by our sounds and 60 per cent by our body language. In empathic listening, you listen with your ears, but you also, and more importantly, listen with your eyes and with your heart. You listen for feeling, for meaning. You listen for behavior. You use your right brain as well as your left. You sense, you intuit, you feel. Listening adds breadth and validity to the decision making of the manager. And by listening to people the manager learns how to deal with them, how their mind works and their approach to problems. The leader must remember that it takes two to speak the truth, one to speak and another to hear. Aristotle's logos, pathos and ethos thus, are three classical touchstones against which we can always test our leadership communication and derive meaningful learning for improving the effectiveness of our messages.

REFERENCES

Barrett D. J. (2006), *Leadership Communication.* New York: McGraw Hill International Edition. 7-12, 85-86.

Carizon, J. (1989), *SAS Video.* Video-taped speech at Harvard Business School.

Cogner J. A. (1998), *The Necessary Art of Persuasion.* Harvard Business Review, May. 85-95.

Dutton J. R, & Ashford S. E. (1993), *Selling Issues to Top Management.* The Academy of Management Review, 18 (3). 397-410.

Fine T. S. (1992), *The Impact of Issue Framing on Public Opinion: Toward Affirmative Action Programs.* Social Science Journal, 29 (3). 323-335.

Harriman B. (1974), *Up and Down the Communication Ladder.* Harvard Business Review, September issue. 144.

Kanter R. M., Stein B. A., & Jick T. D. (1992), *The Challenge of Organizational Change.* New York MacMillan. 244.

Lawson-Tancred H. C. (1991), Aristotle's *The Art of Rhetoric.* London: Penguin Books. 17.

Northouse P. G. (2003), *Leadership -Theory and Practice.* California: Sage Publications Inc. 1-14.

Roosevelt F. D. (1933), The First Fireside Chat, *The Banking Crisis,* March 12, Length 13:51.

Shakespeare W. (1598), Play *Love's Labour's Lost,* Act 4, Scene III.

Sussman L. (1999), *How to frame a message: The art of persuasion and negotiation.* Business Horizons, 42 (4). 2-6.

Sussman. (1999), *How to Frame a Message: The Art of Persuasion and Negotiation.* Business Horizons. July-August.Thoreau H. D., http://en.wikipedia.org/wiki/ReaJity (Dated: 19th March 2007).

BIBLIOGRAPHY

Axelrod A. (2002), *Elizabeth I CEO: Strategic Lessons from the Leader Who Built an Empire.* New Jersey: Prentice Hall Press.

Bass B. M. (1990), Bass and Stogdill's Handbook of Leadership: Theory, Research, and Managerial Applications. New York: Free Press.

Bennis W. (1999), *The Leadership Advantage.* Leader to Leader, Spring Edition.

Bridges R. (1936), *The Poetical Works of Robert Bridges.* London: Oxford University Press.

Bryman A. (1992), *Charisma and Leadership in Organizations.* Newburry Park, CA: Sage Publications.

Buffet W. E., & Cunningham L. A. (1998), *The Essays of Warren Buffet: Lessons for Corporate America Summary.* Denmark: SOS Free Stock.

Butler H. E. (1920-1922), Quintilian's *Institution Oratorio.* Published in the public domain.

Drucker P. F. (1996), *The Leader of the Future.* San Francisco: Jossey-Bass. Gardner J. (1990), *On Leadership.* New York: Free Press.

Hickman O. R. (1998), *Leadership and the Social Imperative of Organizations in the 21st Century. In Leading Organizations: Perspectives for a new era.* Thousand Oaks: Sage Publications.

Lawson-Tancred H. C. (1991), Aristotle's *The Art of Rhetoric.* London: Penguin Books. Mintzberg, H. (1973), *The Nature of Managerial Work.* New York: Harper & Row. Rost J. C. (1991), *Leadership in the 21st Century.* New York: Praeger

Stewart T. A. (1997), *Intellectual Capital: The New Wealth of Organizations.* New York: Currency.

Toffler A., & Toffler H. (1980), *The Third Wave*. New York: Bantam Books.

Lawrence D. H., Greenspan E., Vasey L., & Wosthen J. (2003), *Studies in Classic American Literature*. Cambridge (U.K.): Cambridge University Press.

Durant W. (1961), *The Story of Philosophy*. New York: Pocket Books.

Nohria N., & Harrington B. (1993), *Six Principles of Successful Persuasion*. Boston: Harvard Business School.

Thucydides Warner R., & Finley M. I. (1954), *Pericles' Funeral Oration in The History of the Peloponnesian War*. London: Penguin Books.

Gardner H. (1995), *Leading Minds: An Anatomy of Leadership*. New York: Basic Books.

Covey S. R. (1990), *The Seven Habits of Highly Effective People*. New York : Fireside.

6

Communication for Management Teaching & Research in the International context

*Abha Rishi**

ABSTRACT

In today's globalized world, management students need to understand the complexities of communication in the context of a multicultural and multilingual workplace or the organization's international scope and cultural heterogeneity. Just as employees vary in their national, ethnic and religious backgrounds, so does their perception of communication. Learning about the customs, beliefs and practices that make up a foreign culture's fabric can lead to a better understanding of what the same things can mean for different people. Yet it may be difficult to discern countless cultural distinctions – some of which are subtle – to determine what communication style would be most appropriate for a particular message.

KEYWORDS : Globalized World, Multicultural Workplace, Multilingual Workplace, Cultural Heterogeneity.

INTRODUCTION

"For this reason, top management may often choose to delegate communication to regional managers, who then

---

* Faculty, Laxmi Devi Institute for Engineering and Technology, Alwar, Rajasthan.

style their messages in a fashion that best suits local culture", Hecker says, citing American Standard's management as an example.

In other instances, management may wish to address employees directly in a uniform fashion without differentiating styles, such as when issuing a personal note from an executive to all employees or when communicating highly important matters with company wide implications.

Professor Albert Mehrabian's communications model established this classic statistic for the effectiveness of spoken communications:

– 7% of meaning is in the words that are spoken.
– 38% of meaning is paralinguistic (the way that the words are said).
– 55% of meaning is in facial expression.

Mehrabian's model above has become one of the most widely referenced statistics in communications. *However, it is arguably on occasions applied in an overly simplistic or indiscriminate manner.*

The model is particularly useful in illustrating the importance of considering factors other than words alone when trying to convey (as the speaker) or interpret (as the listener) meaning but care needs to be taken when considering the context of the communication.

Style, expression, tone, facial expression and body language in Mehrabian's experiments did indeed account for 93% of the meaning inferred by the people in the study. *But this is not a general rule that you can transfer to any given communications situation.*

The understanding of how to convey (when speaking) and interpret (when listening) meaning is/will always be essential for effective communication, management and relationships. But using the Mehrabian percentages is not a reliable model to overlay onto all communications scenarios, especially in the multicultural context.

Mehrabian's model is a seminal piece of work, and it's amazingly helpful in explaining the importance of careful and appropriate communications. Like any model, care must be exercised when transferring it to different situations. Use the basic findings and principles as a guide and an example - don't transfer the percentages, or make direct assumptions about degrees of effectiveness, to each and every communication situation.

In his book "Beyond Culture", anthropologist Edward T. Hall distinguishes between low-context and high-context communication. His analysis finds that people of low-context cultures verbalize much of the background information explicitly, since they are not well informed on subjects outside their own interests. In high-context cultures, a great deal of the background information is implicit and requires reading between the lines, with the assumption that message recipients are well informed on many subjects.

Every organization has its own unique culture based on the traditions and value set of its members, which come across in their beliefs, attitudes, priorities and behavioral norms, which is what all management students and their educators should take into consideration while talking of communication, as ultimately they have to step beyond the halls of learning into the organizational workplace.

This paper is based on the CRITICAL THEORY , which has been a distinguishing feature of the communication research program at the one of the Management Schools in Australia, but significant reflection is required to translate the theory into meaningful classroom experiences. The need for reflection comes from two key tensions in teaching management communication: one is the tension between teaching practical, career-focused skills versus critical and/or interpretive analysis; the second is the multicultural classroom environment where students, educated in a monocultural context, are exposed to other interpretations and critiques of their own cultural predispositions and values.

THE CRITICAL REFLEXIVE FRAMEWORK

Our goal as educators is to empower students to participate effectively in both the organizations and communities in which they reside. To achieve this goal while managing the tensions identified above, we embrace a framework of critical reflexive practice (e.g., Cunliffe, 2004). We mean critical to suggest both the sense of questioning, as in "critical thinking," as well as in the sense of critical theory – unmasking hidden tensions and meanings with a goal of emancipating thinking and action (e.g., Alvesson & Deetz, 2000). By reflexive, we mean an awareness of, and questioning of one's own assumptions and constructions of reality.

This framework embodies three underlying principles. The first is that knowledge is both socially constructed and competing. As teachers, we want students to "question assumptions and taken-for-granted actions, think about where/who [they] are and would like to be, challenge conceptions of reality, and explore new possibilities" (Cunliffe, 2004, p. 411).

The second principle is *praxis*, the process of putting theoretical knowledge into practice. While praxis usually refers to the process of putting theoretical knowledge into practice, the strategic and organizational usage of the word emphasizes the need for a constant cycle of conceptualizing the meanings of what can be learned from experience in order to reframe strategic and operational models. *Jung (1994) defined praxis as the need for self-conscious and ethical actions where individuals question their past behavior as well as future possibilities.* Students need to draw on their lived experiences and values while attending to interpersonal relations, communication, conflicts, feelings, and politics. In management communication education, praxis encourages students to reframe past behavior and, by linking to theory, to open up new possibilities for management practice. Thus, we are teaching students a process of reflection and analysis for future action.

The third underlying principle is a critique of values and culture, especially those of the dominant culture. Students analyze and discuss the broader social, cultural, and political issues and critically deconstruct them in light of management communication theory and practice.

The critical reflexive framework requires a teaching methodology that employs tools such as dialogue, decentering, and experiential learning. Dialogue is an exchange of ideas among teachers and students—a moment where we become "struck" by an idea, so that we are then moved to change our ways of talking and acting (Cunliffe, 2004). Dialogue and critical thinking requires students to think more humanistically about the impact of their actions as they are learning (Freire, 1972; Pezone & Singer, 1997). In management education, dialogue is a central way of connecting the individual with the whole organization (Senge, 1992). In classroom practice, dialogue is promoted by positive student/teacher relationships and classroom activities that promote learning opportunities (Brookfield & Preskill, 1999; Giroux, 1987).

The second tool, decentering, aims to provide opportunities for students to recognize conflicting perspectives on a topic, and that the truth is something that is socially constructed (Bean, 2001). Through role play and readings that expose different voices, and by challenging insights through dialogue, students are required to adopt a standpoint on a topic that is different from, and sometimes contradictory to, their own beliefs.

Finally, experiential learning can create opportunities in which students experience conflicting values and perspectives, are forced to make and question choices, and then reflect on the assumptions and constructions that led to their choices. Such tools enable students to realize that there are no "right" answers to problems.

These principles and tools all lead to critical reflexive practice. As critical/interpretive scholars, we encourage students to question existing power structures, knowledge, and conditions in the wider society (Pennycook, 2001). To achieve this goal, Banks (1991) argued that "we must engage students in a process of attaining knowledge in which they are required to critically analyze conflicting paradigms and explanations and the value assumptions of different knowledge systems, forms, and categories" (p. 126). Furthermore, Grey (2004) reinforced this style of critical engagement in his call for critical management education. He emphasized the importance of drawing on student (lived) experiences and values while attending to interpersonal relations, communication, conflicts, feelings, and politics. This approach aims to develop managers who demonstrate moral and political responsibility.

The critical reflexive framework not only challenges students but also challenges us as educators to evaluate how we teach management communication. It is also useful for managing the tensions we see as central to our teaching of management communication in the management programs.

APPLYING THE FRAMEWORK

In the following sections, three critical incidents are presented and discussed how the tensions are reflected in these critical incidents. It is then described how the teacher's response to the incident reflects the principles in the framework of critical reflexive practice and what further possibilities the framework presents.

Critical Incident 1: Using Dialogue

In an executive MBA class where students were examining corporate identity, a student challenged the notion that an organization, when developing an identity strategy, should aim for consistency in messages—a notion that is prominent in the corporate identity literature (e.g., Olins, 1989). He argued that his organization did not have consistency of message and yet the stakeholders were all satisfied with the messages they were receiving. Rather than defend the consistency view, the teacher encouraged the questioning. In the ensuing discussion among students and teachers, the consistency approach was further challenged.

After that session, the CEO of the student's employing organization was contacted and a project established to understand exactly the meaning in the messages that the organization was sending out to its stakeholders. The researchers found that the strategy was based on consistency but that consistency occurred at the level of brand values and not in content communicated or presentation of message (Leitch & Motion, 1999). This was an important finding for the study of corporate identity.

This critical incident demonstrates the critical-practical tension where students and teachers challenged understandings of corporate identity through dialogue. Students, by drawing upon their lived experiences, challenged established understandings of corporate identity as well as the theoretical perspectives the teachers had put forward. In being "struck" by an idea, students and teachers were able to reframe their understandings. By engaging in critical reflection and analysis, they could develop further possibilities for how they thought about management theories and practices.

The incident led to further reflections and possibilities, including an action learning approach. In addition, the dialogue enabled students to engage in cultural critique of the theory and readings from the perspective of their own Asian-Pacific business practices. Students viewed the critiques as salient because they had evolved from their own lived experiences.

Faculty later used the incident as a teaching example of how dialogue can contribute to scholarship. Readings from faculty publications were then used in the management programs and provided students, who had minimal work experience, with examples of theory and cases that applied to the contemporary multicultural business world.

Critical Incident 2: Using Praxis

The second critical incident arose when students in a public relations course felt frustrated with materials that seemed too theoretical and devoid of practical value to their future careers (which is the case with most of our management schools). Furthermore, a focus on critical reflection had led students to question contemporary practices to such an extent that some no longer wished to work in the field of communication, especially in public relations. When students were asked to analyze and apply critical discourse theory, they questioned whether any practitioner used the theory and how practitioners reconciled a critical understanding of public relations with the practical requirements of the role.

The incident reflects the critical-practical tension. Students expected to learn practical, career-focused skills, whereas the teacher's goals were to bring a critical and/or interpretive analysis, through the application of theory, to practice. To resolve this tension, the teacher invited a number of practitioners to participate in a panel discussion with the class. The teacher and students were thus able to explore the implications of critical theory for practice. The practitioners, alumni of the department, first talked about how they used such theory in their campaign work; then reflected on some challenges they had encountered; and finally explained how an understanding of critical discourse analysis, for example, had helped them understand and resolve the challenges.

The incident reflects the critical-practical tension. Students expected to learn practical, career-focused skills, whereas the teacher's goals were to bring a critical and/or interpretive analysis, through the application of theory, to practice. To resolve this tension, the teacher invited a number of practitioners to participate in a panel discussion with the class. The teacher and students were thus able to explore the implications of critical theory for practice. The practitioners, alumni of the department, first talked about how they used such theory in their campaign work; then reflected on some challenges they had encountered; and finally explained how an understanding of critical discourse analysis, for example, had helped them understand and resolve the challenges.

The incident illustrated the value of praxis, as students were able to critically reflect on alternatives to practice and, as a result, see new directions for public relations practice. The teacher could bridge the gap between students' desires for materials that are vocationally oriented and teachers' commitments to critical pedagogies (Pennycook, 2001). Above all, the outcomes from the incident reinvigorated students' interests in working in the industry.

The incident presents further possibilities for teaching and learning. Bringing in practitioners enables the teacher to adopt experiential learning by asking students to apply critical discourse analysis to real campaigns. A further activity, where students engage in decentering, may require students, through role-play, to take on the role of a public relations manager or a stakeholder role such as a community member or activist. Enacting a different role enables students to see conflicting perspectives and thus promotes a more complex understanding.

Critical Incident 3: Negotiating Diversity

In the third incident, two New Zealand Maori students related the experiences of their parents who were not allowed to speak Maori in school. Then a Korean student stated that her own mother had experienced exactly the same form of cultural suppression from the Chinese. The revelation of similarities came as a surprise to all the students, but in particular to the Chinese students, who had a different understanding and experience of their history and who felt uncomfortable at what could have been a criticism of them. The Maori students, who had long believed that their culture was alone in their historical treatment by a colonizing power, were fascinated to learn otherwise.

Although this dialogue was initially unsettling for some students, the teacher addressed the issues from a more general and theoretical perspective, rather than allowing any form of specific criticism. Historically, language suppression has been a widely used tool for invading or colonizing people and cultures. People in Wales, for example, describe similar experiences (Jones, 2004). Instead of avoiding the discomfort that existed in the classroom, the teacher used dialogue to expose the students' perspectives of international politics and public relations. That dialogue led to greater understanding of the vital role of language as a source of power in cultural expression and/or suppression. Through this engagement the students were able to understand how experiences, beliefs, values, and identities can be socially constructed and that "they play a role in constituting their [the students'] everyday organizational realities" (Cunliffe, 2004, p. 411).

The incident illustrates the monocultural-multicultural tension as students began to critique their own cultural assumptions and values as well as those from other cultures. This tension raises three challenges for teachers engaging in critical reflexive practice. The first focuses on the teaching and learning climate. Giroux (1997) claimed that students need the classroom to be a safe place where they can "cross ideological and political borders to clarify their own moral visions ... and move beyond cultural borders in order to approach other cultural patterns, interpret them critically and eventually challenge their own common-sensical assumptions" (p. 262). Part of negotiating these borders is creating a climate of trust through positive teacher-student relationships where students and teachers can engage in praxis. The teacher in the critical incident eventually achieved this state.

Second, students must manage face, particularly international students from East and Southeast Asia, where communication is predicated on face-preserving strategies (Gao & Ting-Toomey, 1998). The Chinese students experienced discomfort because they perceived the attack on their culture as an attack on their personal identity (as members of that culture). Such is the case with some management schools- multi-culturalism can be seen inside a class with a fair mix of people from the North, South, East and West of India. A joke made on the accents can be perceived like a personal attack.

The third challenge is managing the dominance of one cultural group over others. Where students feel they have greater cultural license to speak, they may be silencing others. This cultural license may be validated by an over-reliance on British and North American readings. It may also be validated by the privileging of one teaching and learning style over the another. Many of the students, particularly those from East and South, come from traditional learning backgrounds where the teacher holds the power and knowledge. This monologic approach protects the status quo and promotes competition among students. By contrast, a dialogic approach encourages dialogue and communication. Learning is student centered and collaborative, and knowledge is created/co-constructed though reflection and critical thinking (Freire, 1972; Hammond & Gao, 2002). For the Chinese students, critiquing knowledge through reflection and critical thinking was neither a familiar nor an accepted practice, unlike the Maori students who, more recently, have been encouraged to critique colonial practices. The dialogue also enabled the students to see how knowledge had been socially constructed according to the history of the respective cultures.

CONCLUSION

All three critical incidents illustrate the value of critical reflexive practice as a framework for teaching management communication. Embedded within the framework is the need to question knowledge, to engage in praxis, and to critique our understanding of culture and values within the classroom. Through the tools of dialogue, decentering, and experiential learning, teachers and students can "examine critically the assumptions underlying [their] actions, the impact of those actions, and from a broader perspective, what passes as good management practice" (Cunliffe, 2004, p. 407).

As Guilherme (2002) argued, in practice, it is not a question of depriving teachers and students of truth, certainty, accuracy, and completeness but of offering ideals and principles, showing directions and possibilities, and providing ways and methods for empowerment. Critical reflexive practice enables us to focus on communication rather than persuasion, on empowerment rather than assertion. In addition, this framework helps us to develop managers/practitioners who demonstrate moral, social, political, and cultural responsibility. It can help us infuse students with "civil aspirations"—to have higher expectations of the world and their role in it, "to courageously navigate the moral potholes," and to recognize the world's resources are finite (Giacalone, 2004, p. 419). They need to be able to participate effectively in a society that is increasingly messier and more complex (Grey, 2004).

Teachers and students need to engage in dialogue to allow the emergence of different perspectives, admit when we are unsure of the answers, and critique all types of knowledge and values. Through critical reflexive practice, we can prepare students to be effective communicators in a business environment that is increasingly challenging and changing.

REFERENCES

Alvesson, M., & Deetz, S. (2000). Doing critical management research. London: Sage.

Bean, J. C. (2001). *Engaging ideas: The professor's guide to integrating writing, critical thinking, and active learning in the classroom.* San Francisco: Jossey-Bass.

Brookfield, S. D., & Preskill, S. (1999). *Discussion as a way of teaching: Tools and techniques for democratic classrooms.* San Francisco: Jossey-Bass.

Cockburn-Wootten, C., Henderson, A., & Rix, C. (2005). *Learning from the apprentice: An account of action learning in a university department.* Action Learning: Research and Practice, 2(1), 71-78.

Cunliffe, A. (2004). *On becoming a critically reflexive practitioner.* Journal of Management Education, 28(4), 407-426.

Freire, P. (1972). *Pedagogy of the oppressed.* Hammondsworth, UK: Penguin.

Gao, G., & Ting-Toomey, S. (1998). *Communicating effectively with the Chinese.* Thousand Oaks, CA: Sage.

Giacalone, R.A. (2004). *A transcendent business education for the 21st century.* Academcy of Management Learning and Education, 3(4), 415-420.

Giroux, H. A. (1997). *Pedagogy and the politics of hope: Theory, culture, and schooling.* Boulder, CO: Westview.

Grey, C. (2004). *Reinventing business schools: The contribution of critical management education.* Academy of Management Learning and Education, 3(2), 178-186.

Guilherme, M. (2002). *Critical citizens for an intercultural world: Foreign language education as cultural politics.* Cleveland, UK: Multilingual Matters.

Hammond, S., & Gao, H. (2002). Pan Gu's paradigm: Chinese education's return to holistic communication in learning. In X. Lu, W. Jia, & D. Ray Heisey (Eds.), Chinese communication studies: Contexts and comparisons (pp. 227-244). Westport, CT: Ablex.

Holmes, P. (2004). Negotiating differences in learning and intercultural communication: Ethnic Chinese students in a New Zealand university. Business Communication Quarterly, 67(3), 294-307.

Jones, G. (2004). History and status of the Welsh language. Retrieved February 25, 2005, from http://users.comlab.ox.ac.uk/geraint.jones/about.welsh/

Jun, J. S. (1994). Philosophy of administration. Seoul, Korea: Daeyoung Moonhwa International.

Leitch, S., & Motion, J. (1999). *Multiplicity in corporate identity strategy.* Corporate Communications: *An International Journal, 4(4), 193-199.*

Mintzberg, H. (2004). Managers not MBAs: A hard look at the soft practice of managing and management development. San Francisco: Berrett Koehler.

Motion, J., & Weaver, C. K. (2005). A discourse perspective for critical public relations research: Life sciences network and the battle for "truth". Journal of Public Relations Research, 17(1), 49-67.

Munshi, D. & McKie, D. (2001). Towards a new cartography of intercultural communication: Mapping ideas, business and diversity. Business Communication Quarterly, 64(3), 9-22.

Olins, W. (1989). Corporate identity: Making business strategy visible through design. London: Thames & Hudson.

Pennycook, A. (2001). Critical applied linguistics: A critical introduction. Mahwab, N.J. : Lawrence Erlbaum.

Pezone, M., & Singer, A. (1997). Empowering immigrant students through democratic dialogues. Social Education, February. Retrieved October 14, 1999, from http://web4 .searchbank.com

Roper, J. (in press). Symmetrical communication: Excellent public relations or a strategy for hegemony? Journal of Public Relations Research.

Senge, P. (1992). The fifth discipline field book: Strategies and tools for building a learning organization. New York: Doubleday.

Zorn, T. E. (2002). Converging within divergence: Overcoming the disciplinary fragmentation in business communication, organizational communication, and public relations. Business Communication Quarterly, 65(2), 44-53.

7

Gender Differences in the Use of FTAs when Reporting Incidents of UI: An Indian Study

*Asha Kaul**
*Esha Patnaik***

ABSTRACT

The nature of incidents reported for use of UI entails the possible use of FTAs, that is, challenging the positive or negative face of the target to achieve certain desired objectives. Given research evidence on the differences in communication styles between men and women, we examined the possibility of any such differences in the use of FTA in reported speech within an organization.

No significant differences were found between women and men in the use of FTAs. When the target was of the opposite gender as the agent, the latter was more likely to use either bald on-record or on-record with redressive action approach for influencing. In cases where both the interactants were of the same gender the agent generally used FTAs such as on-record with redressive action and solidarity politeness to gain compliance. A combination of UI strategies was employed in such instances.

KEYWORDS : FTA – Face Threatening Act, UI – Upward Influence, Vertical Influence, Horizontal Influence.

* Professor, Communications Area, Indian Institute of Management, Ahmedabad.

** Research Associate, Communications Area, IIM, Ahmedabad.

INTRODUCTION

Gender studies in organizations have gained significance in recent times, with more women entering the workforce. As they move up the hierarchical ladder, the scope for vertical communication across gender sees a simultaneous rise. Research studies have given varying results regarding the similarities and dissimilarities between the vertical communication patterns of the two groups. In this paper we study gender differences in oral communication using a moderating variable, namely Face Threatening Act (FTA), to study reported incidents of upward influence (UI) in organizations.

Influence, in the organizational context, is the process by which a member of the organization attempts to sway the thinking, actions, or decision-making process of superiors, peers or subordinates. Influence can be of two types - vertical and horizontal. Vertical influence is used across the hierarchical structure of the organization. This again is of two types - upward and downward. Through upward influence (UI) the employee tries to exert control over the thinking or decision making of superiors in the organization, while downward influence is that exercised by the superior over subordinates. Horizontal influence is exercised with peers, internal and external customers and other stakeholders in the organization. We have taken UI as the focus of our present study.

Studies on the communication patterns of women and men indicate an observed difference between the two groups in their interaction patterns in general, and specifically in UI. However, the difference may be affected by various situational factors like role relationship, environment and individual differences, rather than gender differences (Mills, 2002). Extending this last mentioned proposition, we analyzed FTAs - a theory proposed by Brown and Levinson (1987) - across genders to identify if they were a product of gender differences or of situational factors.

The objective of this study is to examine possible differences in the use of FTA between men and women while reporting incidents of UI in an organizational context. The paper discusses FTAs as a moderating variable. The role of FTA in successful (or unsuccessful) UI and possible gender differences in its use form the crux of the review presented here and the subsequent analysis and discussion.

REVIEW OF LITERATURE

With a growing number of women joining the corporate sector, communications research is increasingly taking interest in the similarities and differences between the communication patterns of female and male managers (O'Neil, 2004; Wilkins and Andersen, 1991).

Against this background, research on UI gains importance because of the interplay of real and perceived differences across gender, power distance and the likely difference in criticality of the influence goal for the agent and the target. The successful (or otherwise) employment of influence strategies may result in a range of outcomes, from gaining a favorable result to even expulsion. Thus, the employee has to be careful in deciding whether or not to apply FTAs in an act of UI and how to use it effectively.

GENDER

Literature on gender studies has extensively compared the managerial styles of women and men in the workplace. The focus has been more on the differences in styles, rather than their similarities. These differences have been attributed to various reasons such as the work culture (Gersick, Bartunek and Dutton, 2000), self stereotyping (van Vianen and Fischer, 2002; Lamude, 1993), and work attributes. For example, men are generally found to employ direct and assertive influence strategies, while women tend to prefer agreement and pro-social emotional behavior (Johnson, 1976). These differences have been demonstrated both in mixed-sex groups and in same-sex groups (Johnson, Funk and Clay-Warner, 1995).

UPWARD INFLUENCE

UI is the attempt to secure a desired response from someone higher in the formal hierarchy of an organization (Deluga and Perry, 1991; Kipnis and Schmidt, 1988; Liden and Mitchell, 1988). The effective use of UI strategies secures desired results for the subordinate and can be indicative of their level of success within the organization (Thacker and Wayne, 1995; Yukl and Tracey, 1992; Kipnis and Schmidt, 1988).

Kipnis and Schmidt's (1982) Profiles of Organizational Influence Scale (POIS) identifies six main categories of influence strategies - rationality/reason, ingratiation, exchange, assertiveness, coalition and upward appeal. These strategies may be described as follows (Falbe and Yukl, 1992): **Reason** is a direct strategy, based on logic and rationality. The use of reasoning for UI is directly proportionate to the goals and the needs of the agent (Waldera, 1988). **Ingratiation** is an informal tactic (Schilit and Locke, 1982) based on interpersonal attraction, impression management, and flattery (Kipnis and Vanderveer, 1971; Kipnis, Schmidt, and Wilkinson, 1980; Mechanic, 1962). At times employees might even ingratiate themselves with their superiors without intentionally meaning to (Gardner III, 1992). This could take the form of doing something for them or perhaps carrying out some activity not directly a part of the job profile.

The agent makes use of the **exchange** tactic by exchanging favors or bargaining for compliance by the target (Waldron, Hunt and D'Silva, 1993). **Assertiveness** is a direct or 'hard' pressure strategy (Falbe and Yukl, 1992) used when the employees are sure of their expertise and position. **Coalition** refers to influence exerted in a group. The numerical strength of the group builds up majority opinion for the cause. When the subordinate convinces the superior by assuring agreement of higher authorities, it is referred to as **upward appeal** (Schilit and Locke, 1982). This may not be used as a primary tactic, but is resorted to when other tactics fail (Maslyn, Farmer and Fedor, 1996; Waldron, Hunt and D'Silva, 1993).

FTA

Individuals use language, behavior and gestures to present a certain self image to the world (Morand and Ocker, 2003). This self image that is presented to others is called **face** (Adams and Shepherd, 1996). This may be of two types – **negative face**, which is the desire to be distinct with freedom for unimpeded individual action, and **positive face**, that is, the need to be assimilated, treated as equal and a desire for approval (Mills, 2002; Adam and Shepherd, 1996). Face wants arise out of an expectation that people with whom the individuals interact will affirm and maintain their face (Morand and Ocker, 2003).

Both positive and negative face have two types of subfaces – **personal face** or a desire concerning one's social standing, circumstances and relationship; and **social face**, that is, a desire concerning one's personality, property and preferences (Mills, 2002). **FTAs** threaten either the agent's or the target's desire to be accepted (positive face) or their autonomy (negative face) (Knapp, Stafford and Daly, 1986). Positive face may be threatened through negative evaluations such as criticisms, accusations and contradictions, while negative face may be threatened through impeding actions such as orders, advice, requests and expression of anger or even admiration (Knapp, Stafford and Daly, 1986). Negative emotions are generated by a face threat and responses can range from embarrassment and mild irritation to open hostility (White, Tynan, Galinsky, and Thompson, 2004). To reduce the degree of threat to face, interactants may use various politeness strategies (White, 1997) such as, bald on record, on-record with redressive action, solidarity politeness, deference politeness, off-record, and not say anything at all.

The **bald-on-record** approach is used when the interactants know each other well and there is minimum threat to face. Not much effort is put into reducing the impact of the FTA ("Examples from Brown," n.d.; Ferencik, n.d.). The individual may **go on-record with redressive action**. While the directness of the threat to face is not reduced, the language used is toned down to reduce the impact (Morand and Ocker, 2003). **Solidarity politeness** is based on common ground. It minimizes threat through an expression of friendliness and attempts at bridging any gap between the interactants.

Deference politeness is used in case of a serious imposition on the target's face. The agent tries to mitigate it through means such as being indirect, minimizing imposition and asking for forgiveness. **Off-record** uses indirectness and ambiguity to minimize imposition. The agent maintains ambiguity in the request, thus leaving it open for the target to understand the hint and take some action or choose to ignore it without direct confrontation. When the degree of threat to face is very high the agent may **not say anything** at all.

GENDER AND UI

Like stated earlier, more women are entering the managerial ranks, making gender studies important for understanding organizational dynamics and shaping of the work environment. The patterns of functioning of women and men, their similarities and differences govern interpersonal dynamics and ultimate achievement of organizational goals.

Research results have varied regarding gender differences in the use of UI strategies. While some have clearly brought out differences in their use, others see no clear-cut variation in how women and men employ these strategies. Some studies state that women use more indirect means (DuBrin, 1991) as compared with men when trying to influence their superior. In comparison, men tend to employ the direct and hard tactics of reason (Baxter, 1984) and assertiveness (Johnson, 1976). Some researchers found women more effective in UI (Lauterbach and Weiner, 1996) while others found no difference between the two (Carli, 1989; Sagrestano, 1992; Kipnis, Schmidt and Wilkinson, 1980; Yukl and Tracey, 1992). A relevant question is whether differences, if any, are due to inherent differences between men and women or are socially and contextually governed.

GENDER, FTA AND UI

Existing research on UI has been largely conducted from the psychological, sociological and human resource perspective. While UI has been one of the relevant areas in organizational communication research, the medium of use of influence strategies, that is, language, has been mostly a neglected area (Kaul and Brammer, 2004).

Study of FTA in the light of UI offers interesting possibilities. Three factors govern the use of FTA in an interaction between the agent and the target - the relative power distance between the agent and the target, the social distance between the two and the degree of imposition or urgency involved in the act of FTA (Brown and Levinson, 1987, p. 15).

FTAs lend themselves to regrettable messages (Knapp, Stafford and Daly, 1986). The use of FTAs can result in hostile behavior (White et al., 2004). An agent's use of FTA will be minimum or done away with if the threat to the target's face is high. Use of ambiguous language or indirectness (Riley, 1993) tempers or avoids the use of FTA by creating scope for alternative interpretations. Referring to the context in which FTA may be used, Adams and Shepherd (1996) held that the perceived threat to face will be lower when the context in which it is used is a legitimate one.

Examining how interactional and conversational aspects function in organizations, researchers have found social distance, relative power and the degree of imposition inherent in the request govern the use of FTAs (Morand and Ocker, 2003; White, 1997; Riley, 1993). The nature of UI inherently involves a request for compliance that poses a threat to face of the target. There is the possibility of rebuff, rejection, even formal action being taken against the subordinate. Some UI strategies will have a greater possibility of posing threat to face than others. Also, the degree to which the individual will risk threat to face will depend on the importance of the influence goal (Johnson, Roloff, and Riffee, 2004).

Ideally the employee will use tactics that enable continuing in an organizationally acceptable manner. Given the relational and personal support that exists in a superior-subordinate relationship the interdependence is valued even more by both parties and any threat to face in such a scenario assumes greater significance (Adams and Shepherd, 1996).

Women and men have been attributed with different communication strategies. While the male stereotype is direct, aggressive, logical and impersonal, the female stereotype, in comparison, is soft-spoken, compliant and emotional (Baker, 1991). According to Jaffe, Lee, Huang and Oshagan (1995) men have been known to use more aggressive and 'problem-solving' oriented language while women employ more agreement, support and understanding in their interactions. Some research on gender and language show women to be more sensitive to politeness and issues of status than men (Guodong and Jing, 2005). The tendency of women to apologize more often (Jaffe at el., 1995) also supports this finding. However, the differential effects due to the sex of the agent and the target in same sex and cross sex dyads have to be examined (Brown and Levinson, 1987, p30) more extensively to provide any conclusive evidence regarding interaction patterns in such dyads. Besides, gender and language cannot be assumed to have a direct one-to-one correspondence (Gardner-Chloros and Finnis, n.d.). Gender being a socially and culturally shaped construct, the role of other social and environmental factors will affect the use of language across gender. The type of talk, rather than the gender per se (Gardner-Chloros and Finnis, n.d.) will govern the use of various communication strategies.

FTA can be operational in any act of interaction or communication. Disagreeing, asking for a favor, requesting for information or service, can all amount to a threat to face (Morand and Ocker, 2003). Positive tactics are based on an assumption of commonality of background of the agent and the target. Negative tactics are limited to the situation itself. In negative tactics, the agent may employ indirectness to gain compliance. Positive tactics can actually pose greater threat to face since they are based on the pre-supposition by the agent that there are certain commonalities between the two parties, an assumption that may not be shared by the target. Negative face recognizes the use of an imposition and attempts to moderate it through the use of indirectness and other linguistic means. The organizational and work culture, power distance in the organization and nature of interaction will play significant roles in the choice of tactic used to maintain face.

We wanted to examine if any difference exists across gender of the agent in the use of FTA while reporting incidents of UI. We adopted the method of reported speech for the collection of primary data. Given the sensitiveness of such interaction, recording and/or the presence of an observer would have affected the authenticity of the process. The respondents' narration of the interaction of UI was based on their interpretation of how the interaction progressed, rather than objective documentation of the conversation. The purpose was to capture the intention, the overall process of interaction and the result of the interaction. Parts of the dialogues from the transcripts were qualitatively analyzed to study the likelihood of threat to face in the interactions.

METHODOLOGY

A study was conducted in the western zonal office of an Indian bank which has a ratio of 60:40 of men and women employees. Data was collected from a sample of 109 respondents, with 22 being women and 87 men. They all worked in managerial positions. The length of work experience ranged from zero months, that is, employees who had no work experience, to six and half years. About 22.7 per cent had a degree in management.

Practical difficulties arose in collecting data through direct observation or taping (video or audio) incidents of UI in real situations. Interviewing people, who have engaged in such interactions, met this requirement. A qualitative analysis of the data, to study likely differences across gender in the application of FTA when employees engage in UI was done. The broader objective of studying communication patterns made a qualitative research approach suitable for capturing the nuances of such an analysis.

Primary data by the interview method was collected. The respondents were asked to recall and narrate a critical incident where they had engaged in an act of UI with either a female or a male superior. They were asked to describe briefly the purpose of the influence attempt, what they said or did to influence the superior and how the superior responded to this attempt. They were encouraged to cite examples of or quote what the superior had said.

An examination of the incidents narrated revealed that the issues mentioned were routine, procedural and not critical strategic issues. The issues raised were identified as: difference of opinion, work load related to audit, viewpoint related to bank functioning, customer related, getting leave/ work timings, and coming up with suggestions.

The transcripts were divided into four categories with the objective of studying gender differences if any, in the UI process.

a. Male agent and female target
b. Male agent and male target
c. Female agent and male target
d. Female agent and female target

Each transcript was assigned a code and all identification details were masked. Coding was done for male and female agents and targets, the strategies employed, and the context in which the interaction was carried out. Based on Kipnis and Schmidt's (1982) classification of UI strategies, the reported UI incidents were classified into the following categories: reason and logic, upward appeal, assertiveness, coalition, ingratiation, exchange, and a category of 'others' that included combination tactics. Each transcript was studied to identify the UI strategy used in the instance narrated. At times, the respondents used more than one strategy to gain compliance. These were listed separately, each time a particular approach was encountered in the reported speech. Strategies that did not find a pure fit in any of the six types were classified under the broad heading of 'others' strategy.

SCOPE OF STUDY

The study was conducted in one Indian organization. There was expected to be a degree of similarity in how the respondents addressed the influence situations as organizations have a general prevailing organizational and work culture that governs the general interaction and communication patterns.

The issues discussed for the use of influence were routine organizational issues. Again, a degree of homogeneity was expected to exist in how employees of one organization approach superiors based on the organizational culture.

The sample size taken for the study precludes the generalization of the findings. The findings are indicative rather than representative of the general organizational situation. Cross validation through quantitative analysis will provide more insight into how women and men use FTAs during organizational interactions.

RESEARCH QUESTIONS

In the following section, two primary research questions that address the present study on gender differences in the use of FTA when reporting acts of UI should be explained:

1. What is the impact of threat to face in the choice of UI strategy in different-gender dyads?
   a. What is the impact of threat to face on the choice of UI strategy when the agent is male and the target female?
   b. What is the impact of threat to face on the choice of UI strategy when the agent is female and the target male?
2. What is the impact of threat to face on the choice of UI strategy in same-gender dyads?
   a. What is the impact of threat to face on the choice of UI strategy when the agent and target are both males?
   b. What is the impact of threat to face on the choice of UI strategy when the agent and target are both females?

ANALYSIS

Four transcripts for discussion were selected, which

typically represented the strategy found to be most frequently used in each agent-target combination. The transcripts were randomly picked out from each of the four combinations. Only parts of the narration of the respondents were selected. The texts have been reproduced without any grammatical or language changes. As English is a second language for the respondents, there were many errors which have been reproduced in the excerpts in the interest of maintaining the authenticity of the text. Additionally, as the concern revolved around the verbalization of the influence attempts rather than assessment of the capability in responding in the English language, it was decided that the text be used in its original form.

An attempt was made to identify instances in which FTAs were involved and to see if there was a direct correlation between FTAs and choice of UI strategies across employees of both gender in the organization.

There have been research (Jaffe et al., 1995; Baker, 1991) differences in the use of FTAs and politeness between women and men. However a study of the same while applying UI strategies made it an interesting and challenging area of study.

The following section will:

- Present a table listing the strategies and the reported percentage of use of UI strategies.
- Produce a sample text drawn from the transcripts reporting use of UI strategies.
- Explain the context, analyze the text, and explain the UI strategy and FTA used.

A similar treatment has been meted out to the four different combinations of agent and target, that is agent - male, target -male; agent - male, target -female; agent - female, target -male; and, agent - female, target - female.

In the analysis the agent was referred to as respondent, as the study has been conducted on reported use of UI in critical incidents.

Research question 1: What is the impact of threat to face on the choice of UI strategy in different-gender dyads?

Research question 1a: What is the impact of threat to face on the choice of UI strategy when the agent is male and the target female?

Table 1a: Respondent – M

Strategies	*Target – F* *Reported usage (in percentage)*
Reason and logic	45
Upward Appeal	12.15
Assertion	9
Coalition	11.79
Ingratiation	0
Exchange	0
Others (use of experience and exposure, fact revelation, connection, target gratification and instrumental dependency)	14.06

Context: The trainee officer (male) approached his senior officer about a transaction error. According to him, the mistake was made by the bank officials and not by the customer, and hence, they should rectify the error. The superior (female) was hesitant to do so without adequate documents from the processing department. Through presentation of documents and past transactions the trainee officer was able to convince his superior to adopt the proposed step.

Respondent: I am handling the salary section also. If the account number does not tally to the customer's name, we are parking their salary into some office account temporarily. After getting confirmation in writing from the office, we will credit to their customer account. Once I know the customer through day-to-day interaction, I know this is his account number and the one written by the department is wrong. However, *[name]* madam said that we should wait for written confirmation from the department. Then I went through the entire history of the customer and showed her that we are crediting the salary into that account number. I took photocopies of the sheets of the salaries on the basis of that I made her agree finally.

Application of UI strategy: The subordinate made use of *reason* by offering supporting data, to convince the superior to carry forward a certain line of action. He had his facts ready when he went to meet his superior. He expected some amount of opposition as it involved paper work which had to be cleared by another department. On resistance, he produced the necessary documents to show that an error had been made in entering the account number, for which the customer should not be penalized.

Use of FTA: In this example, the *on-record with redressive action* approach has been used to gain compliance.

During an interaction for UI, the subordinate has to take care to avoid or minimize threat to the superior's face (Riley, 1993). Here the subordinate approaches the superior and asks her to change the decision to hold back the salary payment. The initial attempt is to have her agree merely by providing convincing talk. When she insists on written documents he produces past records in support of his argument. There is a threat to the positive face of the superior. Insistence to change a decision already taken, poses threat to face by pressurizing the superior to comply with something not originally agreed upon. Conviction on the part of the subordinate that they should not be penalizing the customer, even though the superior did not agree, made him apply a more compelling UI strategy. When telling her did not help, he made use of supporting evidence to back his request. The threat was minimized by shifting focus from a personal opposition to compliance based on data.

Research question 1b: What is the impact of threat to face on the choice of UI strategy when the agent is female and the target male?

Table 1b: Respondent - F

Strategies	*Target - F* *Reported usage (in percentage)*
Reason and logic	44
Upward Appeal	24
Assertion	8
Coalition	8
Ingratiation	0
Exchange	0
Others (use of experience and exposure, fact revelation, connection, target gratification and instrumental dependency)	16

Context: The cash verification officer had to report to the manager, finance department, about the daily transactions. Earlier there was no cut-off time for cheque deposits, which made her wait till late evening to clear all the paperwork before leaving for the day. She talked with the manager about setting up a fixed time schedule so that work could proceed faster.

Respondent: We receive so many cheques. Even a Rs. 5/- cheque needs to be entered, you need a printout of that. I used to tell him that there should be a cut-off time to receive cheques that is to be entered the same day. One cannot sit till 8 pm because I have to go to *[another city]*. So I need to convince him.

Interviewer: So he was convinced. How much time did it take for you to convince him?

Respondent: It took almost a month.

Interviewer: All the time you were trying to convince him. You knew that one day he will be convinced.

Respondent: Because ultimately I am sitting late. After the daily ledgers are completed I have a back-up file to be done… and I have to sit just for the processing part so that the back-up files are picked up in *[the regional center]*. … when I went on leave for a month *[the manager]* had to sit and then he realized that this was time wasting and if a cut-off is created it will be much easier.

Application of UI strategy: The respondent tried to convince her superior by *reasoning* that maintaining an all-day ledger entry procedure prolongs their working hours. She is aided in her UI attempt by circumstances which enable her to show her superior the difficulty of her position. She tried to convince him by reasoning that maintaining an all-day ledger entry procedure prolongs their working hours. He was not thoroughly convinced till he experienced the situation himself. The personal experience convinced him of the practicality of what she had been saying.

Use of FTA: A combination of *on-record with redressive action* and *deference politeness* is used to mitigate threat to face.

The subordinate has a better alternative to the current practice but does not push her case too strongly. She prefers to leave the final decision to the discretion of the superior. That is why it takes nearly a month for the manager to come around to what she had initially proposed. Then too the decision is partly influenced by the manager's personal experience in the subordinate's position.

Research question 2: What is the impact of threat to face on the choice of UI strategy in same-gender dyads?

Research question 2a: What is the impact of threat to face on the choice of UI strategy when the agent and target are both male?

Table 2a: Respondent – M

Strategies	*Target – F* *Reported usage (in percentage)*
Reason and logic	26.02
Upward Appeal	21.80
Assertion	9.52
Coalition	14.14
Ingratiation	0
Exchange	0
Others (use of experience and exposure, fact revelation, connection, target gratification and instrumental dependency)	28.52

Context: The senior manager came to know about an anonymous mail sent against an employee to the regional office. He met the regional head to clarify that this could be an internal act of personal rivalry and should not be taken seriously enough to initiate action against the employee without adequate verification.

Respondent: Some customer had written a nasty mail about one of our employees – a complaint which was not true. There were some issues involved in it. So he sent mail to our top people in *[regional]* office and to enquire a committee was set up. This was at the *[name of local center]*. It was decided that a harsh action be taken. We had to discuss on it. If anyone comes and says anything, one should produce proof when a customer has written an anonymous e-mail. If customer is true, send mail to the customer and tell him. Otherwise, just like that, any employee might have written. We did a lot of enquiry.

I told *[the regional head]* to find out the facts before taking action, because first we should know who the customer is, what happened for him to write such a letter, etc., or at least, the customer should give his name, telephone number, etc., so that we could contact. The customer has given some reference saying that he knows such and such person, and it has gone to *[regional]* office. How does a normal person come to know the email ID – may be an internal person was involved in it. I have gone and checked at the *[name of another local branch]* as he had said that he had some relatives in *[last mentioned]* branch, and so on. Everyone there denied that they do not know any operations of that kind. I went and told *[the regional head]* that I have enquired and it seems the claim is a false one, and if action is initiated, it will make someone's life miserable. I suggested that he should call the customer and enquire or drop the case, and tried to impress upon him.

Interviewer: How long did it take for you to convince him?

Respondent: Two or three days, lot of running around.

Interviewer: Then he saw your point of view?

Respondent: After my verifying with the *[name of the other local branch]* branch, I was confident that no such things could have happened.

Application of UI strategy: The attempt is to influence the regional head to change his decision based on *logic*. The manager realizes that they may be spoiling an employee's career by taking disciplinary action against him without adequate proof. He offers his argument to the regional head but is not successful. At his position the regional head may not have had the time to look into all the details of the case (Gabarro, 1979). So the manager does some fact finding to verify the truth of the accusations that have been made against the employee. His enquiries show that there is no basis to what the anonymous mail has claimed. The strong evidence in support of his argument casts a doubt on the authenticity of the accusations and the case is dropped.

Use of FTA: The approach used in this example is that of *bald on-record*.

The threat to face is greater because the subordinate is questioning the judgment of the superior in taking a hasty decision. Earlier literature (Morand and Ocker, 2003) shows that this approach is used mostly when both parties are quite well-known and close to each other and the threat to face is minimum. Here, though it is a formal interaction and the power distance is more, the manager's seniority in the organization lends credibility to his opposition.

Research question 2b: What is the impact of threat to face on the choice of UI strategy when the agent and target are both female?

Table 2b: Respondent – F

Strategies	*Target – F* *Reported usage (in percentage)*
Reason and Logic	38
Upward Appeal	12.5
Assertion	12
Coalition	95
Ingratiation	0
Exchange	0
Others (use of experience and exposure, fact revelation, connection, target gratification and instrumental dependency)	39

Context: The junior officer requires her reporting officer's approval for validating a customer's claims. In one case, the junior thought the papers were not in order so she requested her senior not to pass the application. The latter was hesitant as the customer was a major client. However, through some tactful fact-finding the junior officer found her hunch to be correct and the claim was rejected.

Respondent: For validation we need to take the approval *[of the senior]*. But there is a genuinity as far as the case was concerned *[she was concerned about the genuineness of a particular case]*. So I told her that we have to check this straightforward with the person and ask whether this could be done. This is like offending a customer or something. Then we worked out how we talk about it to the customer without actually offending him and getting the details. It was difficult to tell him because he is a valued customer. He may withdraw the entire amount. A good amount would be lost. We spoke to the person in a way that he not only put in more money, he gave us exactly the details. We saw some of the discrepancies in the data we had. We did not give him the approval, of course. But what he was claiming was not right. We found out that what he was claiming was wrong.

Application of UI strategy: A *combination* of strategies – appeal to ethics and collaborating with the superior - was used to convince the reporting officer to reject the claim. There was the use of persuasion through appeal to ethics and legality of procedure. Since the person was a major client of the branch, direct confrontation was not possible even when they doubted the veracity of his claims. The officer had to be told about how the customer will be handled tactfully during the verification of information. Handling the matter capably was also important since the result would have reflected on the caliber of the reporting officer. While there is no use of coalition as a strategy in convincing the superior, the subordinate uses consensus with the superior to get the work done her way (Floyd and Wooldridge, 1992).

Use of FTA: The *on-record with redressive action* and *solidarity politeness principles* were employed to convince her that this was not a personal issue and they could work together to get over the problem.

The threat to the positive face of the superior (Knapp, Stafford and Daly, 1986) makes the situation sensitive. She was not ready to directly confront the customer since had they been proved wrong, it would have affected the deposits in the bank. The subordinate outlined the approach they can adopt with the customer for verification without turning him off.

DISCUSSION

Much of the research referred to for this paper indicated some difference in the way women and men use FTAs in conversations and interactions. Guodong and Jing (2005) found women to be more polite and sensitive to status than men. The general trend of research findings has been that women are more polite, use more indirect communication strategies and are compliant as compared to men. However, the degree to which women and men will engage in communication that poses a threat to face cannot be determined merely on the basis of establishing a one-to-one relationship between gender and FTA. Various moderating variables will play a role in determining how much of threat to face an individual will risk in an interaction.

Scant literature was available to us on the interplay of gender and FTA in the organizational context. An empirical study based on UI, as the purpose of interaction was thought as the first step towards bridging this gap. UI, by its very nature, involves some degree of threat to the positive or negative face of the individuals concerned. Direct or hard strategies like reason and logic, upward appeal and assertion pose greater threat to face than the softer approaches as they openly challenge the decision of the superior. The softer techniques leave scope for the target to choose, to ignore the influence attempt and also for the agent to avoid through ambiguity an uncomfortable situation.

The transcripts show that in many of the instances narrated, the respondent was found to have used more than one strategy to gain compliance. However, during the interview the respondent named one or the other strategy as the only one to have been used. This can be attributed to the methodology of data collection, that is, reported speech, which lends itself to secondary interpretation rather than primary observation. The present work finds support in literature that a configurational approach to influence, that is, a combination of strategies is more representative of the pattern of influence actually followed in organizations (Farmer and Maslyn, 1999). Falbe and Yukl (1992) argue that it is actually difficult to identify individual strategies since the subordinate is likely to use a combination of more than one tactics for successful UI.

In the previous section we took samples to illustrate how the FTA is incorporated into an act of UI in the four combinations of dyads. A detailed examination of the study results gives further insight into patterns of use of FTA during UI across gender.

Table 5: Comparison of the use of UI strategies in the four female and male dyads

Strategies	*M-F (% of use)*	*M-M (% of use)*	*F-M (% of use)*	*F-F (% of use)*
Reason and logic	45	26.02	44	38
Upward Appeal	12.15	21.80	24	12.5
Assertion	9	9.52	8	12
Coalition	11.79	14.14	8	95
Ingratiation	0	0	0	0
Exchange	0	0	0	0
Others (use of experience and exposure, fact revelation, connection, target gratification and instrumental dependency)	14.06	28.52	16	39

When the agent and the target were of opposite genders, reason and logic was the strategy most likely to be used to gain compliance. While much of the earlier research shows women to use softer or indirect strategies of UI (DuBrin, 1991), here they used direct and hard tactics as much as men, if not more, to influence the superior. Reasoning was considered objective and result oriented. Statements such as, "I used to convince him that as there are lot of ladies already there...", "...if I am there for the presentation, the result would be better", "...a lady approaching a lady would be more effective and comfortable", "I also used to give him statistical data and make him agree for my being there for the presentation", illustrate the use of realistic and practical arguments to influence the superior. Reason and logic is generally used when the threat to face is lower (Waldera, 1988) and the agent can use the bald-on-record approach (Morand and Ocker, 2003; "Examples from Brown", n.d.; Ferencik, n.d.) for gaining compliance. The threat is to the negative face of the target, since the issue has more to do with the situation rather than any personal characteristic of the interactants.

Upward appeal came across as an accepted practice amongst many of the respondents. As one of them explained, the work culture encourages them to be open with their superiors. This reduces the strict adherence to hierarchical formalities and makes the working environment more open. Possibly, the open organizational culture encouraged employees to approach higher-ups with issues if they did not get resolved at the department level. From the perspective of use of FTAs, upward appeal poses threat to the positive and negative face of the target. In several instances, even when the respondent did engage in upward appeal, it was done with the knowledge of the immediate superior or by keeping the latter in the information loop. At times, the subordinate and superior approached the next higher-up together in order to sort out the difficulty (Maslyn, Farmer and Fedor, 1996).

When the agent and the target were both male, then a combination of strategies was used, marginally more than reason and logic, to gain compliance. Men found it easier to convince their male superiors when several approaches were combined for better effect.

Coalition found heavy usage in the F-F combination.

This will find support in literature which propounds that women favor softer, cooperative methods of work (Jaffe et al., 1995; DuBrin, 1991) as compared with aggressive and competitive ones. Thus, they are more likely to use solidarity politeness during acts of UI. Coalition may have been used by itself, or in combination with other strategies to influence the superior.

Interestingly, none of the four agent-target combinations (M-F, M-M, F-M, and F-F) reported the use of ingratiation and exchange for UI. The Indian socio-cultural norms attached to doing work for a senior, whether by age or rank, may explain why ingratiation is not considered as a strategy to be used consciously for influencing. Subordinates may undertake personal assignments on behalf of the superior, not because it may accrue some benefits in the future, but because it is part of the cultural ethos. If we were to apply the same socio-cultural pattern to exchange, in the traditional Indian hierarchical structure the superior or senior is the one who 'gives' and the subordinate 'receives'. Exchange breaks this pattern by assuming a relationship based on equal give-and-take from both sides.

In contrast with earlier literature that found that men use more hard or direct tactics (Baxter, 1984; Johnson, 1976), assertion was the least frequently used of all the strategies, whether the agent and the target was a woman or a man. This is reflected by the difficulty in identifying it in the scripts under study. An understanding of the term as taking a stand and then pursuing it with reason and logic was definitely found in all the scripts. However, it was never in isolation but always in combination with reason and logic, which happens to be the most frequently used strategy in the data available.

Content analyis of the UI situations narrated during the interviews gave an indication of the likelihood of an FTA being employed in any of the four agent-target combinations.

The results may be extrapolated as follows:

Table 6: Extrapolations From the Study

Strategies	*M-F*	*M-M*	*F-M*	*F-F*
Bald-on-record	✓	✓	✓	✓
On-record with redressive action		✓		✓
Solidarity politeness				✓
Deference politeness			✓	
Off-record		✓		
Say nothing at all	The threat to face is too high for the agent to engage in UI			

Bald-on-record was used in all the dyads, though not as the primary strategy. While many respondents used reasoning for influencing, given the importance attached to save face, agents found it inappropriate to directly confront the target with facts and reason. Usually, bald-on-record was softened by combining it with some other strategy. Same-gender dyads employed on-record FTA with redressive action for gaining compliance. On-record FTA with redressive action was employed in many of the cases, as an extension of the importance given to hierarchies in many organizations in India. Interestingly, this strategy was used only in the same-gender dyads. Quite likely, as the bonding in same-gender dyads was higher than in mixed-gender dyads, the agent attempted to use positive politeness by mitigating the threat to face of the target by resorting to redressive action. As Baxter (1984) argues, "greater politeness" exists in relationships involving close friends.

A combination of UI strategies was used in same-gender dyads, rather than a single strategy. When one approach did not work, the agent adopted another, till the desired response was elicited. The F-F dyad favored the use of solidarity politeness for successful UI. The present study gave limited evidence of deference politeness being used in any of the dyads. Only the F-M dyad provided some scope for this approach to be used. Examples of such patterns are dependent on the social factors in the use of language, which are reflected in the use of honorifics (Brown and Levinson, 1987). Similarly, off-record was found to have been pursued only in the M-M dyad. Respondents in this category mentioned meeting their superiors outside the workplace in social or organizational gatherings where they dropped a hint of what they wanted to be done. As "outside the organization" meetings and partying are more common for men in the Indian context, the UI is attempted indirectly "so that the meaning is to some degree negotiable" (Brown and Levinson, 1987).

In our study, women respondents did not narrate any instance where they tried to influence their superior outside a formal interaction. Application of FTAs in such situations, therefore, did not arise. The same was the case in instances where the agent was a male and target female.

CONCLUSION

The present study throws up interesting dimensions to the study of interactional patterns across gender. Some earlier studies (van Vianen and Fischer, 2002; Johnson, Funk and Warner, 1995) found inherent differences between women and men in their patterns of interaction. The aim of the present study was to explore if this difference translates into a difference between the two in the use of FTAs. The results of the present study indicate that FTAs are not gender specific in acts of UI. They are more contextual and governed by the organizational culture and the social context of the participants. One of the reasons that can be attributed for this result is the nature of tasks reported while recalling incidents of UI. As stated earlier, the tasks described related to routine work. In routine tasks, the threat to face is low as the interplay between individual and interpersonal dynamics determines and establishes a pattern for and of organizational interaction.

In the organizational context, there is more of an 'organizationally fit' pattern of communication that is used. This is based on the organizational and work culture and established patterns of communication across hierarchies. It will be erroneous to state that merely the gender of the agent or the target impacts the choice of words used to save 'face'.

DIRECTION FOR FUTURE RESEARCH

As gender diversity in the workplace gains importance, the emphasis on interactional pattern of women and men in the workplace becomes more relevant. To the best of our knowledge, hardly any work has been done to study the interplay of gender and FTA in the context of UI. This creates the space to conduct further studies in the field and gain a macro perspective to the subject.

The use of reported speech for interactional analysis is a new approach which does not find much mention in the literature that was accessed for this paper. While there are limitations to the narrative method, such as accuracy of recall and degree of subjectivity, employing this technique for data collection will enable researchers to examine organizational situations where direct observation is not possible. Combining this technique with other approaches will also help in cross-validating data and exploring other dimensions to the subject.

Expanding the study to several organizations across industry sectors will bring out the role of diversity and organizational culture in the use of FTAs by women and men in their choice of UI strategy.

REFERENCES

Adams, Carey H. and Shepherd, Gregory J. (1996). Managing volunteer performance: Face support and situational features as predictors of volunteers' evaluations of regulative messages. *Management Communication Quarterly, 9*(4), 363-388.

Baker, Margaret Ann (1991). Gender and verbal communication in professional settings. *Management Communication, 5*(1), 36-63.

Baxter, L. A. (1984). An investigation of compliance-gaining as politeness. *Human Communication Research, 10*(3), 424-456.

Brown, Penelope, and Levinson, Stephen C. (1987). *Politeness: Some Universals in Language Usage*. Cambridge, UK: Cambridge University Press.

Deluga, Ronald J. and Perry, J. T. (1991). The relationship of subordinate's upward influencing behaviour, satisfaction and perceived superior effectiveness with leader-member exchanges. *Journal of Occupational Psychology, 64*(3), 239-252.

DuBrin, Andrew J. (1991). Sex and gender differences in tactics of influence. *Psychological Reports, 68*(2), 635-646.

Falbe, Cecilia, M., and Yukl, Gary (1992). Consequences for managers of using single influence tactics and combinations of tactics. *Academy of Management Journal, 35*(3), 638-652.

Farmer, Steven M. and Maslyn, John M. (1999). Why are styles of upward influence neglected? Making the case for a configurational approach to influences. *Journal of Management, 25*(5), 653-682.

Floyd, Steven W. and Wooldridge, Bill (1992). Managing strategic consensus: The foundation of effective implementation. *Academy of Management Executive, 6*(4), 27-39.

Gabarro, John (1979). Socialization at the top: How CEOs and subordinates evolve interpersonal contracts. *Organizational Dynamics, 7*(3), 3-23.

Gardner III, William L. (1992). Lessons in organizational dramaturgy: The art of impression management. *Organizational Dynamics, 21*(1), 33-46.

Gersick, Connie J. G., Bartunek, Jean M., and Dutton, Jane E. (2000). The importance of relationships in professional life. *Academy of Management Journal, 43*(6), 1026-1044.

Johnson, Danefle Ifert, Roloff, Michael E., and Riffee, Melissa A. (2004). Politeness theory and refusals of requests: Face threat as a function of expressed obstacles. *Communication Studies, 55*(2), 227-238.

Johnson, Cathryn, Funk, S., and Clay-Warner, J. (1995). Organizational contexts and conversation patterns in same-sex task groups. Paper presented at the annual meeting of the American Psychological Association, Washington D.C.

Johnson, Paula (1976). Women and Power: Toward a theory of effectiveness. *Journal of Social Issues, 32*(3), 99-110.

Kaul, Asha, and Brammer, Charlotte D. (2004). Study of Speech Act Theory in upward influencing in an Indian workplace. Proceedings of the 2004 Association for Business Communication Annual Convention.

Kipnis, David and Schmidt, Stuart M. (1988). Upward-influence style: Relationship with performance evaluations, salary, and stress. *Administrative Science Quarterly, 33*(4), 528-542.

Kipnis, David, and Schmidt, Stuart M. (1982). Profiles of organizational influence strategies (Form M). San Diego, CA: University Associates.

Kipnis, David, Schmidt, Stuart M., and Wilkinson, Ian (1980). Intraorganizational influence tactics: Explorations in getting one's way. *Journal of Applied Psychology, 65*(4), 440-452.

Kipnis, David, and Vanderveer, Richard (1971). Ingratiation and the use of power. *Journal of Personality and Social Psychology, 17*(3), 280-286.

Knapp, Mark L. Stafford, Laura, and Daly, John A. (1986). Regrettable messages: Things people wish they hadn't said. *Journal of Communication, 36*(4), 40-58.

Lamude, Kevin G. (1993). Survivors' upward influence tactics in same-sex and cross-sex dyads. *Perceptual and Motor Skills, 77*(3), 1067-1070

Lauterbach, K. E., and Weiner, B. J. (1996). Dynamics of upward influence: How male and female managers get their way. *Leadership Quarterly, 7*(1), 87-107.

Liden, Robert C. and Mitchell, Terence R. (1988). Ingratiatory behaviors in organizational settings. *Academy of Management Review, 13*(4), 572-587.

Maslyn, John M., Farmer, Steven, M., and Fedor, Donald, B. (1996). Failed upward influence attempts: Predicting the nature of subordinate persistence in pursuit of organization management. *Group and Organization Management, 21*(4), 461-480.

Mechanic, David. (1962). Sources of power of lower participants in complex organizations. *Administrative Science Quarterly, 7*(3), 349-364.

Morand, David A. and Ocker, Rosalie J. (2003). Politeness theory and computer-mediated communication: A sociolinguistic approach to analyzing relational messages. *Proceedings of the 36th Hawaii International Conference on System Sciences (HICS)*. IEEE.

O'Neil, Julie (2004). Effects of gender and power on PR managers' upward influence. *Journal of Managerial Issues, 16*(1), 127-144.

Riley, Kathryn (1993). Telling more than the truth: Implicature, speech acts, and ethics in professional communication. *Journal of Business Ethics, 12*(3), 179-196.

Sagrestano, Lynda (1992). Power strategies in interpersonal relationships. *Psychology of Women Quarterly, 16*(4), 481-495.

Schilit, Warren K. and Locke, Edwin A. (1982). A study of upward influence in organizations. *Administrative Science Quarterly, 27*(2), 304-316.

Thacker, Rebecca A. and Wayne, Sandy J. (1995). An examination of the relationship between upward influence tactics and assessments of promotability. *Journal of Management, 21*(4), 739-756.

van Vianen, Annelies E. M. and Fischer, Agneta H. (2002). Illuminating the glass ceiling: The role of organizational culture preferences. *Journal of Occupational and Organizational Psychology, 75*(3), 315-337.

Waldera, L. M. (1988). A study of key variables related to the directness of upward influence strategies and to self perceptions of upward influence. *Dissertation Abstracts International*, 50, 02B.

Waldron, V. R., Hunt, M. D., and D' Silva, M. (1993). Toward a threat management model of upward communication: A study of influence and maintenance tactics in the leader-member dyad. *Communication Studies, 44*, 254-272.

White, Judith B., Tynan, Renee, Galinsky, Adam D., and Thompson, Leigh (2004). Face threat sensitivity in negotiation: Roadblock to agreement and joint gain. *Organizational Behavior and Human Decision Processes, 94*, 102-124.

Wilkins, Brenda M. and Andersen, Peter A. (1991). Gender differences and similarities in management communication: A meta-analysis. *Management Communication Quarterly, 5*(1), 6-35.

Yukl, G. and Tracey, J. B. (1992). Consequences of influence tactics used with subordinates, peers and the boss. *Journal of Applied Psychology, 77*, 525-535.

Yukl, G. (1998). *Leadership in Organizations*, fourth edition. Upper Saddle River, NJ: Prentice-Hall.

Web links

Examples from Brown and Levinson's politeness strategies (n.d.). Retrieved on 13 February 2006 from http://logos.uoregon.edu/explore/sociol-ing/strat.html.

Ferencik, Milan (n.d.). Pragmalinguistics and stylistics. A Survey of English Stylistics. Retrieved on 13 February 2006 from http://www.pulib.sk/elpub/FF/Ferencik/10.pdf.

Gardner-Chloros, Penelope, and Finnis, Katerina, (n. d.). Code-switching, gender and politeness: A study in the London Greek-Cypriot community. Retrieved on 5 December 2005 from http://webs.uvigo.es/ssl/actas2002/07/06.%20Penelope%20Gardner.pdf.

Guodong, Liang, and Jing, Han (2005). A contrastive study on disagreement strategies for politeness between American English and Mandarin English. *Asian EFL Journal, 7*(1). Retrieved on 13 February 2006 from http://www.asian-efl-journal.com/march_05_lghj.php.

Jaffe, J. Michael, Lee, Young-Eum, Huang, Lining, and Oshagan, Hayg (1995). Gender, pseudonyms, and CMC: Masking identities and baring souls. Paper submitted for presentation to the 45th Annual Conference of the International Communication Association, 1995, Albuquerque, New Mexico, USA. Retrieved on 13 February 2006 from http://members.iworld.net/yesunny/genderps.html.

Mills, Sara (2002). Rethinking politeness, impoliteness, and gender identity. Gender identity and discourse analysis, 69-89. Retrieved on 5 December 2005 from http://www.linguisticpoliteness.eclipse.co.uk/Gender%20and%20Politeness.htm.

White, Ron (1997). Minding your maxims. Retrieved on 13 February 2006 from http://www.rdg.ac.uk/app_ling/maxims.htm#E% 20text.

8
WAC: A Teacher's Perspective

Niraj Kumar *

ABSTRACT

Written Analysis and Communication (WAC) is among the highest ranked courses in the functional area of communication in post graduate management curriculum in India. The course is basic in nature where students are guided to sharpen their analytical skills through written communication. At the outset, it is important to make clear that this is neither a course on written communication nor on case analysis methods. This course, uses these tools to achieve the objective of the course, i.e., 'honing analytical skills' which are indispensable for any manager.

It is true, that the course is still not a 'regular and common' course in most of the management institutions. However, this is so because the course demands a specialized skill and very high involvement and time from the concerned faculty. Lack of qualified faculty in "Communication" area is another reason why this course is not being offered in its 'true' form. Although, some of the leading management institutions in country where faculty members are available, this course is being offered and is being managed with the help of academic associates, with the involvement of more than one faculty members, or with the help of WAC readers.

KEYWORDS : Written Analysis, Communication, Learning

* Faculty, Rural Management Xavier Institute of Management, Bhubaneshwar

IMPORTANCE

The course, besides teaching students to think, analyse, and make decisions in rational and logical way, also provides opportunity of writing various forms of managerial written communication which managers either make use for their own decision making, or to communicate their decisions so that messages are understood and acted upon as expected by the writer. As the course is offered in the beginning of programme, it helps students to learn various approaches of case analysis as means of learning tools, and aims to instill the habit of making decisions based on facts and on given situations.

The course meets the direct and fundamental expectations of recruiters, that, potential managers should have good analytical and writing capabilities. Strategic written communication is one skill which is most sought after by various recruiters and the course provides such opportunities to develop those skills.

Students from diverse academic backgrounds join a management programme. The course, as it progresses, inculcates a habit of rational and logical analysis of written facts or /and information and then to re-organise the contents for an effective communication. By providing a framework for analysing and writing, the course successfully guides every student to develop a specific style of professional working required by the managers.

PEDAGOGY

The best way to achieve the objectives of this course is to make students work on their own after the teacher provides some basic guidelines and pre-requisites for analyzing written communications including case studies. The contents are suggestive in nature and participants are expected to use their own wisdom, experience, and other sources of information for learning. There are more than one ways of analyzing written communications, at the same time one can be effective by writing in more than one ways. Level of teacher's involvement and amount of time required for this course are quite high. Assignments of each student need to be evaluated judiciously with all possible constructive criticism so that student may work on it and bring improvement. Level and type of input (content) given to the students, and the pedagogy would vary with the specialization students are going to do during their two year's course. If the students are of sectoral management programme like, environment and forest management, development management, rural management etc. the content would be specific to their specialization and different than those having courses in general management programme. However, there are many situations when it does not work and teacher has to adopt prescriptive pedagogy and use more structured content defying the basic tenet of the course.

a. When there is wide variation among the students either in their intellectual capabilities or in their English writing skills. This creates two different 'groups' of students within a given class; one which learns fast and the other not able to cope up. The former brings and wants variations in learnings while the latter wants prescriptions to work on. If teacher promotes the first group, second group is left out and loses it's confidence and motivation. Prescription model would certainly help the students of second group but this would discourage innovativeness and diversity in learning styles.

b. When overall quality of students is very low, students expect examples to follow and try to replicate teacher's suggestions. This defeats the purpose of the course as the pedagogy becomes prescriptive in nature.

c. If the time available to students is not sufficient then they will not able to work on the assignment, as it is required, to have self learning. Secondly, 'last minute approach' in which students start and complete the work under deadlines, does not help in learning from the course and it becomes more mechanical and structural.

THE CASE

WAC, one of the core courses of full credit (30 contact hrs), is offered in the first term of two year's PG Diploma in Rural Management (PGDRM), at Xavier Institute of Management, Bhubaneswar (XIMB). The course has two major parts, namely written analysis and written communication. The written analysis part aims at developing the analytical skills and logical decision making skills; where as, written communication part aims at developing skills in effecting written communication. The course is being offered to PGDRM students since last three batches.

Although, case analysis is major means of dealing with the first part of the course, analysis of other publications, like, annual report, occasional reports / papers, in-house magazine, sponsored publications in different regular magazines from different organizations are also used. Students are expected to go through these publications and analyze and present it (in written form) as per the instructions in assignments given to them. In written communication they are facilitated to develop skills in writing common managerial communications. Usually, they are expected to work in collaboration with any organization / corporate offices and develop some communication materials for them. Preparing project proposals and project reports for Orissa based development organization are most common outcome of students' work.

The teaching style has largely been dependent on factors like, number of students in class (it has varied 40 to 62), average quality of students (this too has varied from batch to batch), and time available with the faculty (number of course/s he had in a given term). Students were informed about the various components/ assignments, their respective weightage, expected dates of submission, etc. as soon as they registered with the course. They were also provided with some on-line reading materials on each assignment (hard copies were made available on request). There were introductory sessions when the assignments were introduced with basic information about the assignment, expected outcome, and some 'pre-requisites / must be' of the assignments. Students were encouraged to refer as many sources as possible for more information related to their assignments. After a student submitted his/ her assignment it was evaluated and commented upon by the faculty regarding strengths and weaknesses of the assignment with suggestions to further improve upon. Students were also given opportunities to clarify doubts and seek suggestions if they so desired. There was a session for overall feedback by the teacher where he broadly shared his overall opinion and suggestions about the assignment. There were few remedial measures which were taken to help those who were found lagging behind. However, the gap remained till the end. It is important to mention that concerned faculty had brought changes (like, giving another assignment similar to that which has already been evaluated and commented). Although, in every batch some of the students were found using innovative approaches on working on assignments, but most of them remained dependant on the reading materials provided to them or tried to go along the examples given or discussed in the class.

The final feedback of the participants remained very encouraging for the concerned teacher but the teacher was of view that the course could not achieve its objectives as it should have been. Students realized that the course was useful and had helped them in learning analytical and writing skills. Some of the limitations which teacher realized were more students centric were like we know all syndrome, easy to work on communication assignments, lack of consistency in performance. Some of the experiences worth mentioning are:

* The quality and level of students changed the basic objectives of the course and it turned towards a written communication course as the quality and level went down.
* The workload on a teacher was quite high, and if assignments were evaluated by some body else then how to maintain uniformity (WAC readers or faculty associate were temporary and left the job after a year or so).
* Evaluation became difficult when there were wide differences among the students as far as their written skills were concerned. The disparity between the students from a rural background and those from convent schools makes the task tougher and some times students who had put more efforts and had shown improvements got less mark than those who simply had better English writing capabilities.
* Students did not repeat the performances and so were not able to make learnings as a part of their professional behavior.

Almost all concerned with the course, like students, alumni, teachers, recruiters, agree that the course is very important and the way it is being taught is an effective way of dealing with such courses. However, there is still a lot of scope of improvement in handling this course. It is important to understand that it is not just another course of management and the course has longer and wider implications for a manager, and so, it requires a more concerted effort from the discipline (Communication) to make this course more effective. Teachers too require some training in dealing with this course.

9

Reflections on Communication & Extension Courses for Forest and Natural Resource Management

*K. N. Krishna Kumar**

ABSTRACT

Communication science in 21st century has emerged as one of the foremost integrated and application oriented subject. The wide range of applications of communication science in this modern world has made its study truly integrated, with research input from social, behavioral, physiological, political, extension, and soft & hard ware aspects of telecommunication and IT sciences. Role of communication in management need not be elaborated. To be a successful manager, one has to be essentially a good communicator. This is true with respect to management of human as well as natural resources that include forest and others. Realizing this fact, full fledged discipline, with qualified and faculty in the field of communication and extension was started in early 90s at IIFM to offer courses on communication methods and extension with special focus on forest and natural resource management.

Currently, IIFM offers two educational programs two years PG Diploma in Forest Management (PGDFM) and one year Post Master-M.Phil. level course on Natural Resource

* Professor, Indian Institute of Forest Management, Bhopal

Management (NRM). Together, five courses on communication methods and extension education are being taught in these two programs. While the courses related to Communication methods focus on business, organization and written communication skills, the Extension education courses emphasize on community mobilization / participation and transfer of technology with reference to development sector. The teaching is based on cases generated through faculty research along with fair number of class room as well as field exercises.

Periodical assessments of student's performance are carried out through pre-determined evaluation pattern. Feedback on the course taught is taken from the students at the end of the term through independent institutional mechanism and communicated to the concerned faculty. The feed back received on communication and extension Students are provided with course out line in a pattern, prescribed format, which contains learning objectives, session wise topics, internal & guest faculty, evaluation references etc. at the beginning of the course. Feed-courses had so far been constructive and constantly helped to revise and update the content and pedagogy of the courses over the years.

KEYWORDS : Communication, Development, Management, Forest and Natural Resource Management.

Preamble- Study of communication in management

Communication is an essential input in socialization and social process at all levels. It makes a society dynamic and determines its behaviour. Culture and behavioral patterns are transmitted from one generation to another within a society through communication. Communication is age old science, since the beginning of human civilization and Aristotle was the one who initiated the systematic study of art of communication by postulating the first module of communication. His 'Speaker-Speech-Audience' module, though a linear one, was the foremost to begin the systematic study of communication process. Since then, we have come a long way to this IT era and sure to keep going, in a much faster phase to attain new heights in communication technology and its application for societal development. However, overwhelming majority of all the technological developments in communication have occurred during the later half of twentieth century. Due to this, the speed with which we communicate has been changing rapidly. Now almost everything can be heard or seen as it happens in real time. A striking illustration of the extent to which communication speeded up, specially because of technological advancement in telecommunication can be provided by comparing two significant events in the world history. Almost one and half century ago, in 1865, the British Government learned about Abraham Lincoln's assassination 12 weeks after the event; a century later, in 1969, it just took 1.3 seconds for us to hear as well as see Neil Armstrong, the first man landing on the moon. As the telecommunication brought the societies across the countries together to create 'Global village', now rapid advancements in IT has made it a 'Global family' through virtual communication .

The field of communication has not merely advanced in technological front over the years. While virtually nullifying the distance between the countries through IT, the communication science in 21st century has emerged as one of the foremost integrated and application oriented subject. It would not be exaggeration if it is said that every moment communication takes place at different levels - individual, family, community, society and mass levels of human society. At the country and global levels, communication has become an important aspect of economic and political activities. Individual's and societal behaviors are determined or assessed by their ways of communication. The wide range of applications of communication science in this modern world has made its study truly integrated, with research input from social, behavioral, physiological, political, extension, and soft & hard ware aspects of telecommunication and IT sciences.

The recent advancements in the field of telecommunication and IT have resulted in a quantum change in communication technology, particularly increasing the speed, improving the quality of reception and at the same time decreasing the cost.

Greater understanding in social and behavioral sciences makes easy to effectively relate the content and method of communication to the receivers or the audience. While the integration of such different expertise makes the study of communication as a specialized and complex profession, its application in different fields, especially for knowledge dissemination and for resolving many managerial and human relationship problems is another important side of the coin. Due to this multi-dimensional nature and use, communication becomes an indispensable factor, greatly influencing the effectiveness of any kind of management process, including human and natural resource management. It is needless to say that to be successful manager, one should be a essentially a good communicator and the study of management is incomplete without the study of communication. The purpose of this paper is to share information and experience with regard to communication and extension courses being offered to forest and natural resource management students at Indian Institute of Forest Management (IIFM).

RELEVANCE OF COMMUNICATION & EXTENSION TEACHING IN FOREST & NATURAL RESOURCE MANAGEMENT

The modern concept of forest and natural resource management does not restrict its domain merely to protection and conservation of such resources. Rather it emphasizes on their sustainable utilization and management by the concerned stakeholders. It is now well accepted that management of forests and other natural resources is not the exclusive responsibility of the government, but it is a particicipatory exercise, to be jointly carried out by the direct stakeholders - government, local community and other agencies including NGOs. Obviously, participation cannot occur with out communication, which is also essential for resolving conflicts between the stakeholders.

As the forest and natural resource management is getting increasingly linked with promotion of rural livelihood, it has become an important component of community development. Like Development Management, Development Communication is also emerging as a specialized profession, providing information and extension support to the development process. Apart from business and organizational communication, the students of forest and natural resource management at IIFM also acquire development and extension communication skills through core courses, which help them to get equipped as Development Managers.

COMMUNICATION & EXTENSION COURSES OFFERED AT IIFM

Education, training and research are the core activities of IIFM. Major contents of education and training, including the cases used are being generated through faculty research and hence making them more application oriented. Currently, the institute offers two educational programs PG Diploma in Forestry Management (PGDFM), which is a two years management course and one year long M.Phil level Post masters course on Natural Resource Management, shortly known as NRM.

For PGDFM students, two communication courses and one extension course are being offered. The basic 'Communication Methods (CM)' course of half credit load i.e. 15 classroom sessions in a term is offered in first term. This is followed by a one credit course on 'Written Analysis and Communication (WAC)' in the second term. The 'Forestry Extension (FE)' course of 30 sessions i.e. one credit load is offered in the third term. The NRM participants undergo the 'Development Communication (DC)', a course of half credit load during the first term. In the second term, another half credit course 'Extension Methods (EM)' is offered. In addition, the condensed version of 'Written Analysis and Communication' course with half credit load is offered as elective course during second term.

However, historically, the communication and extension teaching got separate identity in terms of independent courses as described above only after competent faculty joined at IIFM. In case of PGDFM, traditionally, communication was taught as a part of Managerial analysis course (MAC). Managerial analysis, coupled with communication was taught in three spells i.e. in three terms as MAC-I, MAC-II and MAC-III. But in these courses, major focus was on managerial analysis and only minimal input on communication was given. Extension education, which is considered as an essential input for Development management, was totally absent. These lacunas were pointed out during the curriculum review exercises and full fledged, separate courses on communication and extension as mentioned in above paragraph were introduced from 1998 on wards.

COURSE CONTENT, PEDAGOGY & EVALUATION

The major criteria for determining the contents of communication and extension related courses are

- knowledge and skill required for development management with particular focus on forest and natural resource management in the current context.
- general profile and requirement of the jobs being offered to the students through campus recruitment
- knowledge and skill being looked for by the recruiters

— feedback from alumni and recruiters
— recent developments in the field and inputs generated through faculty research.

The pedagogy – method of instruction, in all the courses is a mix of lecture sessions, exercises, group discussions, case studies etc., providing adequate opportunity for class participation. Though reading materials are provided time to time, their objective is to guide and encourage self-learning rather than to promote route learning. Individual as well as group assignments and field visits are important components of course-pedagogy. For instance, the WAC course is entirely assignment based course and the classroom discussions in the FE & EM courses primarily based on the students' mid-course field visits and field work programs.

Course evaluation, like in all leading management schools, is a continuous process. The objective is to provide opportunity for improvement to both, the students as well as teachers. Series of on-course evaluations like objective tests, assignments, mid and end term examinations are built in the course structure. Each evaluation component is assigned certain weightage and all put together constitute 100 per cent. Class participation of individual student is also assessed throughout the course, on many occasions like regular classroom discussions, assignment presentations, group discussions, case study discussions etc., with due weightage.

Detailed course outline for each course, which includes leaning objectives, session wise topics along with teaching faculty, pedagogy, evaluation pattern, available references etc., is provided to the students before starting of the course. Tables 1 to 5 of this paper provide specific course contents of each course.

Specific course content, pedagogy and evaluation pattern of each course are detailed below.

I. Course name : Communication Methods (CM)

Course offered to : PGDFM students during I term

Credit load : 0.5 (15. sessions)

Learning Objectives:

i. Gaining basic knowledge on communication methods useful for effective management.

ii. Getting familiarized with interpersonal, group and written skills essential for business and organizational communication.

Pedagogy : Lecture cum discussions & classroom Exercises

Evaluation : Class Participation, Mid-term assignment & End-term examination

Table 1. Session topics

Sl. No.	*Topics*
I	**Basics of communication**
	i) Concepts and functions of communication
	ii) Communication models useful in management and development.
II	**Communication barriers in management process**
	i) Inter-personal barriers
	ii) Overcoming communication barriers
	iii) Management trainee in trouble-case study
III	**Formal communication Skills – Exercises**
	i) Use of different communication vehicles (forms of communication)
	ii) Getting message across
	iii) Communication grid & field
IV	**Organizational & business communication**
	– Business Communication – an overview
	– Communication Process and types in organizations
	– Team working-Intra and inter team coordination in an or-

ganization – Game exercise

– Written Communication: Basics and Skill Practice

II. Course name : Written Analysis & Communication (WAC)

Course offered to : PGDFM students during II term

Credit load : 1.0 (30 sessions)

Learning Objectives:

i. Improve situation (case) analytical skills for effective decision making

ii. Improve written communication skills for a variety of managerial requirements.

Pedagogy

The course relies predominantly upon case / assignment method of teaching and requires time bound feed back to the students by the teaching faculty. Lectures, classroom discussions and presentations will be used primarily to clarify the concepts related to case analysis and written communication under different managerial situations. Since learning in WAC will be primarily through written reports /assignments and their comprehensive feedback, number of classroom sessions will be only 15 and are spaced out.

Evaluation

The course evaluation essentially constitutes the evaluation of assignments submitted by the students. The course will have no mid / end term examination.

Table 2. Session topics

Session No.	*Topic*	*Assignments*
1.	Introduction & Case writing	
2.	Case analysis	
3.	Case -I	Assignment -I
4.	Case-II	Assignment -II
5.	Popular article	Assignment -III
6.	Research report writing	
7.	Research report writing	Assignment -IV
8.	Case-I feed back	
9.	Case-II feed back	
10.	Article writing	Assignment - V
11.	Popular article feed back	
12.	Report writing feed back	
13.	Business correspondence	Assignment -VI
14.	Article writing feed back	
15.	Business correspondence feed back	

III. Course name : Forestry Extension (FE)

Course offered to : PGDFM students during III term

Credit load : 1.0 (30. sessions)

Learning Objectives :

i. Understanding the relevance and application of Extension Education concepts and methods in forestry & related sectors.

ii. Gain the competence in use of Methods of Extension Education, Extension Programme Planning (EPP) and Transfer of Technology (TOT) with special reference to Participatory Forest Management (PFM).

Pedagogy : Lecture cum discussions, Case studies, Classroom Exercises & Field visits

Evaluation : Class Participation, Pre-mid Term assignment, Pre-mid term quiz, Mid-term examination, Post-mid term assignment & End- term examination

Table 3. Session topics

Sl. No.		*Topics*
I		<u>**Pre-Mid term**</u>
1.	**Introduction to Extension Education**	
	a.	Concept, definitions & need for forestry extension
	b.	Extension (learner centred) education process
	c.	Principle of Extension & key questions case study: Participatory eco-development programs
	d.	Emerging trend in Forestry Extension - Participatory Extension - Farming System (Satellite) approach - Farmer back to farmer (feed forward) approach
2.	**Extension Method**	
	a.	General orientation: inter-personal & group methods
	b.	Application of extn. Methods (in promotion of Group Exercise) - JFM/Community Forestry (CF) - Agro-Forestry - Industrial/Commercial Plantations - Eco-tourism - Watershed development
	c.	Role of folk media in extension work, experience sharing on environmental awareness campaigns by BGVS
	d.	Designing Extension Campaign on identified issues during week-end field visit – group exercise & presentation
3.	**Farm- Forestry Extension**	
	a.	Concept & issues

Case study : Industry-Farmer Interface :
Role of forestry extension

4. **Extension Program Planning (EPP)**

a. Concepts & different (recent) approaches of EPP & steps

b. Application in JFM / CF - Exercise on EPP

II **Post-Midterm**

5. **Diffusion of Innovations**

a. Concepts of social change and diffusion process
Case study : Television set

b. Adopter categories
Case Study: Water boiling in Peru village

c. Attributes of Innovation
Case Study: Transfer of bio-gas technology

d. Innovation-decision paradigm
Case study: Surplus to scarcity – case of contingent adoption

e. Role of change agents in Participatory Forest Management (PFM)
Case studies:
- Scarcity to Surplus:Will JFM show the way:case of Makroda village
- Participatory Institutions:Key to JFM Case of Shampura
- Participatory Forest Fire Management: Case from Western Ghats
- People's Forest:Case from Biloda (Video)
- Board Game for extension agents

6. **Extension Training Management**

a. Participatory training – cycle, need analysis, methods & evaluation

7. **Media Management in extension work**

a. Agenda setting role of media
Case study: Print media role in JFM, special reference to Harda (IIFM-Cambridge Univ. Study)

b. Media management for effective Development- Extension work

c. Preparation & effective use of Development- telecast

d. Preparation of Extension (print) literature

IV. Course name : Development Communication (DC)

Course offered to: NRM participants during I term

Credit load : 0.5 (15 sessions)

Learning Objectives:

i. Gaining basic understanding of communication process and approaches/strategies of development support communication

ii. Learning practical aspects of Development communication process in the context of Participatory Natural Resource Management.

Pedagogy : Lecture cum discussions, Case study discussion, Field visit to JFM/Watershed village to study development communication process

Evaluation : Class Participation, Mid Term assignment, End Term examination

Table 4. Session topics

Sl.No.	*Title of the sessions*
1	i) Communication process – Basic concept
	ii) Perspectives of Development Communication
2	Elements of Development Communication process
3	Models of Development Communication
4	Emerging trends & strategies in communication, their relevance to resource management and development in general
5	Factors affecting fidelity & overcoming barriers in development support communication
6	Television set – Case study
7	Developing Communication skills
	i) Communication, Listening & Group communication quotient – Self assessment exercise

	ii) Communication grid & Communication field
8	Effective team (group) work & inter team coordination in development process – Exercise cum discussion
9	Role of media in development communication
	Media perception & agenda setting with reference to JFM – Research case discussion

IV. Course name : Extension Methods (EM)

Course offered to: NRM participants during II term

Credit load : 0.5 (15 sessions)

Learning Objectives:

i. Conceptual orientation to Extension Education as the process and programme and its relevance to natural resource management.

ii. Gaining familiar to use of Extension methods in promoting participatory resource management.

Pedagogy : Lecture cum discussions, Case study discussion & Field visit

Evaluation : Class Participation, Mid Term assignment, End Term examination

Table 5. Session topics

Sl. No.	*Topics*
1.	Introduction to Extension Education a) Concept & definitions b) Historical perspective & recent trends c) Principle & Key questions Case Study : Participatory eco-development programs
2.	Extension Method a) General orientation: inter-personal & group methods b) Organizing Extention demonstrations & campaigns c) Weak-end field visit to the CIAE-KVKadopted village to study the Extention Work d) Designing Extention Campaign on identified issues during field visit – Group exercise & presentation

3. Extension programme planning
    a) Concepts & steps
    b) Exercise on programme planning
4. Diffusion of Innovations
    a) Concepts of social change and diffusion process
    b) Adopter categories

       Case Study: Water boiling in Peru village
    c) Attributes of Innovations

       Case Study: Transfer of bio-gas technology
    d) Innovation-decision paradigm

       Case study: Surplus to scarcity – case of contingent adoption
    d) Role of change agents in participatory resource management Exercise: Board Game for Extention Agents

---

FEED BACK & CONCLUSION

Objective feed back obtained from students on teaching of the course always helps to improve upon the content, pedagogy, evaluation etc. At IIFM, the students' feed back is considered as an important measure to assess the faculty's effectiveness. Feed back from the students is taken independently by the curriculum cell for all the courses taught at the end of each class room term. The format of evaluation is the same for all the courses of both PGDFM and NRM. Feed back is taken on following parameters, each one assessed on a five point continuum.

1. Lecture
    1.1. Lecture clarity
    1.2. Orderly sequence
    1.3. Adequacy of examples
2. Text books/Poly copy
    2.1. Text book suitability
    2.2. Poly-copy suitability
    2.3. Audio/visual presentation

3. Cases, if any
    - 3.1. Case relevance
    - 3.2. Case effectiveness
4. Projects/Assignments
    - 4.1. Relevance
    - 4.2. Effectiveness
5. The instructor
    - 5.1. Presentation
    - 5.2. Enthusiasm
    - 5.3. Concern for students
    - 5.4. Enforcing discipline
    - 5.5. Adherence schedule
6. Evaluation
    - 6.1. Relevance to coverage
    - 6.2. Timeliness of feedback
    - 6.3. Fairness in evaluation
7. The course as a whole
    - 7.1. Achieving objectives
    - 7.2. Interest evoked
    - 7.3. Overall rating
8. About the respondent
    - 8.1. Your commitment level

In general, all the communication related courses are well rated (4.00 & above) by the students; where as the utility of the Extension course is more appreciated by the alumni than the current students. This may be because the content of the extension course seems simple, but it is mostly practice / application oriented and needs more practical sessions in the field. Usually, exercise/case oriented sessions are well received. More emphasis on written communication and presentation skills is demanded. Participatory teaching, though consumes more time, escalates enthusiasm among students. Application oriented questions, usually asked in the examinations of communication and extension courses are better welcomed than those encouraging route learning.

The overall experience in offering communication & extension courses and feed back show that constant updating of course contents, appropriate mix of pedagogical styles and learner centered approach in teaching, all together help the students to effectively participate in the learning process and achieve the course objectives.

10

Teaching Presentation Skills to MBA Students in a Business Communication Course — a Case study

*Payal Mehra**

ABSTRACT

The paper presents a case-study illustrating the pedagogy applied towards teaching of **Presentation skills** *to prospective management students as part of the Business Communication course in a well known second rung management institute in North India.*

Following a brief introduction of some of the benefits of the course on business communication to prospective management students, the paper then presents the framework for **student-centered learning** *and explores the link between benefits of student-centered learning and the pedagogy followed in the teaching of presentation skills.*

The current pedagogy followed by the instructor was an improvement on the previous one; the new method relied on incremental improvements where the students voluntarily sought to improve his speaking skills and not as an obligation for fulfillment of course requirements. This approach yielded better results in the long run.

KEYWORDS : Presentation Skills, Student Centered Learning, Impact-making Communication.

* Faculty, Jaipuria Institute of Management, Lucknow.

INTRODUCTION

In an MBA course, typically, graduate students are preparing for entry level positions in business, and therefore, need to learn advanced communication skills such as delivering presentations, leading meetings, managing teams, conducting performance reviews, resolving conflicts, writing memos, documents and proposals. The Business Communication course, which essentially deals with these aspects, has been a part of core requirement for business students for many years now. The students are assessed on a variety of communication skills - both oral as well as written.

Of late, a thought is emerging that a typical business communication course taught in the first year should not only be known for its importance in the business setting but also for its effectiveness - the impact this kind of training has on the students to assess and improve their basic skills. Business Communication course must be result oriented in that it must be taught as a skill to be mastered to the best of ones ability. It has become extremely critical to decipher how best to teach communication skills to business students to meet real world standards.

It has been generally observed, that in recent times, graduate students prefer to play a more active role in the class, "challenging text book material, lecture and student comments that contradict their own observations" (Pittenger, et al, 2003). Students with prior work experience tend to have greater insights than the average graduate on most issues relating to the business world. This changing profile of the students demands a more rigorous pedagogy that combines the theoretical input with practical utility.

STUDENT CENTERED LEARNING

Gibbs Y. Kanyongo, (2005) explains the concept of a Student-Centered Approach in the context of teaching learning of advance level courses. According to him, in student centered environments, teaching learning styles involve two aspects - Eestablishing a knowledge base and promoting learning. Instructors typically use content to advance learning outcomes. Weimar (2002) in his study points out that there are three ways in which instructors use content to advance learning outcomes. First, instructors should "use" content, not "cover" content as a vehicle to develop learning skills. Second, content should be used to promote self-awareness. The students should be able to self- assessment of their strengths and weaknesses as learners, and then develop strategies that help build on their strengths and make up for the weaknesses. Third, content promotes learning. In learner-centered environments, active learning strategies should be used all the time. Students should have hands-on learning experiences, not just listen to the instructor explain some concepts. Research also recognizes that students internalize knowledge in different ways and in the context of different situations.

PRESENTATION SKILLS

Most studies on communication show that, though both oral and written communication skills are important in the business world, yet effectiveness in oral communication, especially presentation skills, is rated highly by Indian practicing managers for judging effectiveness in communication skills.

Increasingly, the ability to effectively design and deliver business presentations is acquiring the status of a science as much as an art. Because presentations are delivered orally, under relatively public circumstances, they require few special communication techniques which are taught to students in class. A presentation training is considered useful by the instructor on many counts - it is a comprehensive package which not only deals with effective public speaking but also encompasses areas like information gathering and management, management of time, confidence building, adapting to audience interests, elements of persuasion techniques, and audience handling. Students, on their part, consider presentation training useful as feedback about self is given in a relatively controlled environment and desire to adapt to industry standards is manifest due to the competitive environment created in the class-room.

PRESENTATION-PEDAGOGY

The table presented below gives an overview of the popular pedagogy followed in Indian B-Schools with respect to presentation skill development in students.

Table 1 (about here)

The table above illustrates the pedagogy in general adopted by business communication instructors, to enable the students to acquire appropriate presenting skills. The most effective is the 'workshop approach' where the emphasis is on skill refinement by creating certain context-relevant scenarios giving opportunity to the students to reflect on them. Building awareness among the students about their strengths as well as weaknesses and the desire to create an impact on the audience are some important bases for developing a skill of this kind.

A typical communication course uses the Training Model (see below) to teach the students; however, the traditional model of teaching-learning Business presentations in this institute (See Approach 1) has been modified with a slight variation- prior assessment has been added to obtain an idea about present competency level before any formal training in presentation skills is imparted to the student (See Approach 2). Thus, every student is given at least two opportunities to speak – once before any formal training is imparted to the student and the other, after the training is given by the instructor. At the same time, other faculty members were also encouraged to give maximum opportunities to the students to express themselves in public situations in their respective courses. This approach was devised following complaints from other departments that the students were just not putting enough efforts in enhancing their basic skills (See Chart 1 below).

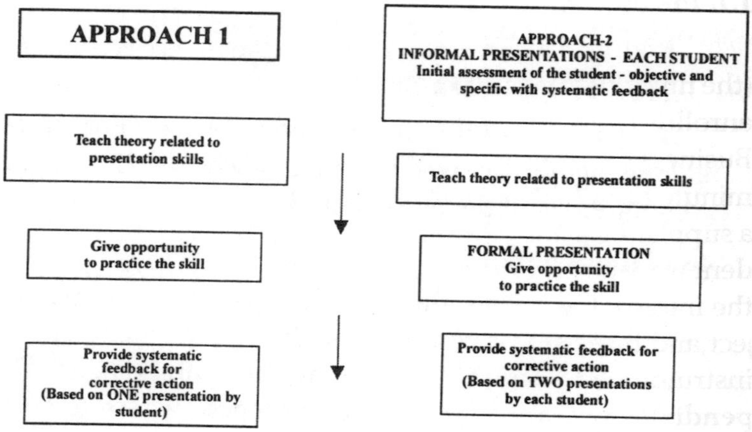

Chart 1 : Example of a Training Model used for Teaching of Business Presentation Skills to Management students in India : Two popular Approaches

1.0. Stages in Presentation Skill Assessment

The first step in designing an effective presentation skill assessment activity for students was to assess the individual merit of the students in public speaking and confidence level **before** any formal presentation training could be imparted by the instructor. It gave an opportunity to the instructor to assess the general communication pattern of the students in the class in a scientific manner and then design a suitably relevant course (a form of customization-which is in essence what good communication, is all about). Secondly, it actively engaged the students early on in their first few days of the semester and made them realize the importance of effective communication in their work lives. Thirdly, a before and after approach helped to scientifically assess the incremental change and possible shortcomings in the instructors style and pedagogy approach. The students also benefit, as they can assess what they originally were in terms of confidence and techniques of presentation and what they have achieved.

1.1. Process

Preliminary Presentations : In the month of July 2005 (the time when students enter the management institute and enroll for the first semester program), the students in the Business Communication course were asked to give a four minute presentation on a topic selected by the student from a supplied list (**Appendix A-1**). For the presentation, the student was selected randomly on any lecture day. In this way, the interest level of the student was maintained in the subject and he/she also got a chance to speak extempore. The instructor used a formal presentation feedback form (**Appendix A-2**) for this exercise and the feedback was returned to the student the next day itself with the grading as well as comments and suggestions for improvement.

At this stage, no discussions were held on how to make a successful presentation.

Table 2.1 (about here)

A feedback exercise was conducted on these sessions. Many students expressed fears with, regards to public speaking. A large number of these fears related to fear of the audience, fear of evaluation and more importantly, the failure to express their views confidently in the English language. This appears to be a quite true in countries like India where there is a wide variation in the way English is spoken and written, largely due to presence of intense regional diversity and prevalence of different education systems. The students also expressed doubts and anxieties related to planning, structuring and presenting the message tailored to a specific audience in a limited span of time. This proved to be the basis for planning the next stage which was the Intervention strategy.

1.2. Intervention strategy

The next stage was the INTERVENTION strategy. The instructor spent *four* sessions of 90 minute duration each on emphasizing the elements of a successful presentation strategy. The instructor highlighted the various aspects relating to presentation skills. A lecture on audience analysis, information management and coordination, body language, voice modulation, confident public speaking, preparing PowerPoint presentation slides and question answer handling was delivered to the students. The students were taught some basics on grammar and sentence construction along with an overview of current usage in business vocabulary. Business English modules were distributed in the class rooms. Inputs related to phonetics and diction were also given. These techniques helped students who were weak in English to adapt to business requirements much more easily. A lecture on impression making and impact making strategies was also delivered to the students. Additionally, inputs on professional attire and business etiquette were also given. The instructor spent considerable time counseling coaching and guiding the students so that they could improve on their previous performance. These proved to be little investments in building confidence among the students.

Students were encouraged to use the real world situations and advised to plan their presentations in such a manner that it was addressed to a (hypothetical) business audience and not necessarily the academic community. Thus, the audience for the students could be clients, professionals, bosses, subordinates union leaders etc. The presentation method suggested was extemporaneous as this method is by far the most popular and effective method. In this method, the student first thoroughly prepares the speech. Subsequently, he prepares notes from the speech that he has prepared. The student usually rehearses, making sure that he has all the parts in mind, but there is no attempt to memorize. "Extemporaneous presentations generally sound natural to the listeners yet they are, or should be, the result of careful planning and practice" (Lesikar).

1.3. Final Presentations

The third stage was the phase of the second presentation round after the formal presentation training. In this phase, students had to work in groups and evaluation was group based. Groups of four students were formed by the instructor and topics were assigned to each group (See **Appendix A-3**). In this phase, group working and team communication norms were also included in the evaluation. Each group was required to discuss the presentation theme with the instructor and submit a presentation plan format (**See Appendix A-4).** A separate evaluation form was used for the group's assessment (**See appendix A-5**). This assessment was also peer-centric and each individual in each group in turn, was assessed by five of their peers as well as by the instructor. Though the marks were given individually to each member of the groups yet a proportion of the marks were also reserved for competency in team communication.

Some ground rules were established-

- The use of podium was discouraged to enable the student to project his entire body language to the audience and hence, be more prepared.
- Use of hand notes was discouraged as it looks unprofessional. Cue-cards were allowed however.
- Formal attire was encouraged. The ladies had to wear saris and the men had to wear formal suits. A short PowerPoint presentation to aid the presentation was an essential prerequisite.
- Strict time management to be adhered to.

One sees that substantial improvement has taken place as many students have recorded an above average score, in contrast to the pre-presentation performance.

Table 2.2 (about here)

The results indicate that considerable improvement has taken place due to the formal presentation training. A preliminary analysis suggested that two aspects may have contributed to the improvement in the students' performance. In the first place, exposure to greater number of public speaking forums proved to be major contributing factor. The second time round the student was a little more prepared, and had also given presentations in few other courses as well, that were simultaneously going on. The fear of the audience appeared to be gradually dissipating. The students were enthused to 'prove their mettle' the second, time such an organized activity presented itself. Secondly, the students, own learning from the discourses in the intervention strategy also was a guiding factor. The next step was to try and find out whether or not this improvement was statistically significant by applying the paired comparison t-test. This exercise in statistics was conducted from a thoroughly academic viewpoint. The test was used as a tool by the instructor, as a barometer to measure her own performance as an instructor of presentation skill development.

It is expected that there would be a significant change in the presentation style of the students after a formal and systematic training is conducted by the instructor.

Hypothesis

The following null hypothesis was tested for 179 respondents of the first year batch of students pursuing a PGD-BA course:

Ho: There is no difference in the scores achieved by the students before and after the technical presentation training of the students. In other words, the impact of the presentation skill training is negligible on the development of this skill in students.

A paired sample t-test was conducted to find out the difference in the pre and post presentation training for batch of 179 students of the first year post graduate program. The significance of the test is .000. This is the p value at 95% confidence interval. Therefore, the null hypothesis is rejected and it is concluded that there exists a significant difference in the pre and post presentation training ratings. This implies that the training has made a difference to student's performance especially in terms of what they originally were and what they aspire to become in terms of presentation delivery. The mean difference in the ratings is 4.65 and this value is statistically significant. The standard deviation is (predictably) high before the training is given (indicating a highly variable performance) and significantly lower after the training, indicating a more standardized performance. (4.46 and 2.97 respectively)

1.4. Interpretation and analysis

The above results indicate that improvement has taken place after a systematic training in presentation skills. Students exhibited keenness to know about the finer nuances of communication, especially body language, and most of them were able to put them into use. Significant emphasis was placed on how to gather and present information so that the presentation gave a focused and well rounded appeal. An emphasis was placed on style as well as substance so that the students lacking in either or both could work on them with help from the instructor. English language background was perceived to be a definite asset while communicating to an audience and the instructor felt that those with vernacular orientation or those who have studied in a medium other than English did have difficulties in presenting. Message planning and delivery (the context as well as content) was laid special emphasis on and by and large, many students worked hard along with the instructor.

The study also revealed that, training, howsoever, intensive cannot produce perfect results, especially in an area like business communication where some disparities are always likely to be there. That is precisely why despite two systematic feedbacks by the instructor and by peers as well as VCD recording, the results are not so perfect and there is sufficient scope of improvement.

Feedback from the students revealed that through this exercise, the students were able to grasp the significance of impact-making communication and the importance of making a good presentation to their careers.

CONCLUSION

As instructors we attempt to understand many aspects of our student population. As in most communication situations, instructors need to be aware of the audience they try to influence, specifically their backgrounds, age profile, competency in written and oral business language and their expectations from the instructor.

Understanding our students has helped us to be more effective in communicating the information we think is relevant for the students in the business world. We are guided by not only our own understanding of what needs to be taught but also by research of what suits a student best in a typical situation such as presentation skill training in this case.

Specifically, answers to the following queries was sought-

- Is the current style of teaching, in this case presentation skills, effective?
- Can the incremental change in the students' presentation ability be measured?

- How far is the student able to comprehend the design (of message) to delivery (of message) approach while presenting?
- What could be the possible shortcomings in the approach of the instructor?
- What future course of action could be adopted to enhance the students' presentation ability?

The present study threw some interesting revelations. There was a marked improvement in the presentation and confidence standards due to the intervention strategy followed by the instructor. This implied that the student centered approach was essential for a course focused on high skill development of the student. Students were given sufficient opportunity to use the content of the course so that they learn and experience it firsthand. Only then were they able to internalize and use the learning for their personal development. This was found to be an effective way in which the students could make an objective assessment about their strengths and weaknesses. In this case, the student was exposed to two public speaking forums in the Business Communication classroom and received continuous feedback throughout pre-training and post training sessions.

Feedback was timely and given in a scientific and organized manner. The self knowledge achieved through feedback allowed the student to work intelligently and effectively in self improvement. This worked well for both the student as well as the instructor. The continuous feedback given to the student helped him to be clear about his strengths and weaknesses and fine tune the areas to improve upon.

Most students tend to think of business presentations as performances, rather than conversations which must impact the audience - touch their mind and hearts. This gap was sought to be reduced and emphasis on message design to message delivery was elaborated in detail. Attention was given on planning the message, coding the message and communicating the message. In other words, students responded positively towards designing presentations which fulfilled a certain purpose.

For an effective utilization of time and energy so that class objectives are achieved, proper planning is necessary for best results. In this case - it included designing of presentation assessment format in the pre-training phase, the training module and designing of assessment formats in the post training phase, well in advance. This included list of functional topics for the groups to present as well co-ordination with videography department for 360 degree feedback.

The present study gave pointers to the course instructor for refining the presentation assessment. It was thought advisable to devise a separate presentation training module for engineers so that their presentations could be made more creative and interesting.

Incoming quality of students is often variable, especially in India, as many students are from vernacular background and not fluent in the English language. With the intent of strengthening the quality levels of all students, the approach taken by the College of Business at Rochester Institute of Technology (RIT) is mention worthy as a similar approach (albeit on a smaller scale) was sought to be replicated in this institute.

Learning from this exercise

The exercise was a tremendous learning experience for the instructor. In the first place, it gave an opportunity to the instructor to gauge the level of the incoming batch of freshman students and customize the training program accordingly. Secondly, the problem-to-solution approach helped the students to be aware of their strengths and weaknesses and improve themselves in the two rounds of presentation assessments that were organized. As the pedagogy adopted was largely student centered, the role of the instructor was more of a facilitator than a tutor of concepts. Since one to one interaction was maintained, the students felt an enhanced sense of responsibility to improve their presentation skills. The instructor was able to assess and counsel the students on two parameters-

1. How do they communicate when working alone?
2. How do they communicate when working in a group?

The first phase of assessment was achieved through solo presentations conducted in the first round and the second phase of assessment was achieved in the second round of group presentations.

Lastly, it may be said that these exercises gave a significant boost to the confidence and morale of the students. A marked improvement was visible in the presentations the students gave to faculty members in other disciplines and a positive impression was created on the recruitment panel who visited the campus for placement interviews. Above all, the satisfaction the instructor achieved is immense in terms of genuine value addition to the students and the instructor.

Limitations of the exercise

It is at times felt that the large batch size may deter the most dedicated of teachers. It is a daunting task to arrange presentations for as many as 180 students twice over in 40 odd hours of total teaching time available to the instructor, and this requires thorough planning and investment of time by the Course Instructor. Many a times the instructor has to juggle between being a professional evaluator and an emotional anchor at the same time. Moreover, students initially tend to consider Business Communication as a soft course and rarely feel the need to take it seriously. Only when the students realize that they really lack good communication skills do they give full attention to this important life skill. Creating this feeling is a challenge and a task which most business communication teachers must strive to accomplish. Only when learning is sought then teaching becomes more exciting. Having the informal presentations at the start of the semester cured the students of the myth of their being perfect communicators and brought them into the track of learning communication skills to their best advantage.

REFERENCES

1. Baker Thompson, Teaching Pr4esentation Skills, Business Communication Quarterly Jun 2004 Vol. 67 Pp216-219
2. Barker Randolph T, Stowers Robert H, Learning from our Students-Teaching strategies for MBA Professors, Business Communication Quarterly, Vol 68,Issue 4
3. Conno, Michael, Orientation through Presentation: Getting MBA students interested in Communications Training, Business Communication Quarterly Dec,2005Vol 68,Issue 4 pp488-492
4. Dyrud, Marilyn A, Worley Rebecca B, Teaching MBA's ,Business Communication Quarterly, December 2005,Vol 68,Issue 4,pp 479-480
5. Gibbs Y. Kanyongo, Teaching an Introductory Graduate Statistics Course Online to Teachers: Preparing to Become Principals: A Student-Centered Approach, International Journal of Instructional Technology and Distance Learning July 2005, and Vol. 2. No. 7.
6. Glenn Wharton, Faculty perceptions of Communication Skills and needs of Business school graduates in Singapore Business Communication Quarterly December 2002Vol 65 pp 39-59
7. Haynes Worley, Dyrud, Strategies for Teaching Business Communication Business Communication Quarterly, September 2002 Vol. 65 pp 86-92
8. Knight Melinda, Communication in Non US MBA programs Business Communication Quarterly, Jun 2005 Vol 68 Issue 2 pp 139-179
9. Levas, Mc Crew, Adams, Assessment Business Communication assignment of English as second language students, Business Communication Quarterly, Vol. 65 pp 30-43
10. Mc Pherson, Bill Student Perceptions about Business Communica-

tion in their careers, Business Communication Quarterly Jun.98 Vol. 61 pp 68-79

11. MM Monipally, Teaching Business Communication, The current Scenario In India, Proceedings of the national Seminar on teaching business Communication at Indian Business Schools, Mar 2001,IIMA
12. Mehra, P, Managers' perception of the Importance of Business Communication for effective job performance: an empirical evaluation, Icfain Journal of Management Research ,September 2005
13. Mergan Erhan Stevenson Williams, Total Quality Management, Sowing the seeds of quality: quality at the source. Total Quality Management, Nov 2002, Vol. 13 ,Issue 7 pp 1015-1020
14. Pittenger, Miller, Mott Using real world standards to enhance students' presentation skills Business Communication Quarterly Sept. 2004 Vol. 67 pp 327-336.
15. Thomas Martha Wetterhall, hardyiv, Samuel B, Communication Instruction in a Mature Institutional partnership, Business Communication Quarterly pp 197- 208
16. Ujvala Rajadyaksha, Teaching of Communication in Business Schools in India, Proceedings of the national Seminar on teaching business Communication at Indian Business Schools, Mar 2001,IIMA
17. Weimer, W. (2002). Learner-centered learning: Five key changes to practice. San Francisco Jossey-Bass.
18. William Wardrope, Department Chairs' perceptions of the Importance of Business Communication Skills Business Communication Quarterly Dec 2002 Vol. 65.Issue 4 pp 60-72.

11

Effective Informal Managerial Communication : An "Open Eye And Ear" Approach

*Sharmila Subramanian**

ABSTRACT

Managerial communication does not restrain itself to corporate presentations, meetings, conferences, media relations, official correspondences like business letters, memos, proposals and reports. This is quite obvious from the fact that today we have "hi-tech" communication like intranet, internet, teleconferencing, video-conferencing, net meeting etc... also as a part and parcel of our professional communicative life. But, communication is not always formal. In fact, informal communication is far more active at the work place than formal communication.

People at workplace spend between ***25% to 70% in face-to-face conversations, and about 88% to 93%*** *in unscheduled communication (Whittaker et al., 1994). This enhances the level of informal communication in the organisations. This type of communication is sometimes backed by opportunity, and sometimes spontaneity. On one hand, it augments mutuality and solidarity, on the other hand it spreads rumours and counters formal communication network. Informal tie ups give rise to cliquey functioning in the organisation, which in turn induces clique*

* Associate Professor, Institute of Management and Information Science, Bhubeneshwer

politics. The consequences can be low productivity, low morale, less belongingness and high attrition. To cope with these problems managers need to adopt "an open eye and ear" approach to organisational communication. The paper attempts to provide a solution to the problem of informal (mis) communication and organisational politics, that is acceptable to both academia and industry.

KEYWORDS : Communication, Rumour Mill, Interaction, Capability.

Communication (both formal and informal) is like blood to any living organisation. Having understood its importance, most of the organisations now make strategies for communicating with their internal employees. Terms like HR communication, internal communiqué, Quality Circle, internal-operational communication, communicating to the internal customers or internal stakeholders have occupied considerable spaces in the policy documents of almost all **** organisations.

Social gatherings, family days, party-time, in-house fun, and open gossip have also started appearing in the organisational agenda these days. All these developments indicate the fact that communication in an organisation is an indispensable function and any attempt to devalue it would run the risk of a total organisational chaos.

Thus, certain organisations have started harnessing informal communication channel, which is far more prevalent and effective than the formal networks.

Tata Metaliks Ltd. has a unique way of developing committed employees; they do it by creating individual task leaders. To make one and all accept these task leaders the HR department utilizes friends and close associates in each informal group. This informal channel of communication, in turn, makes the tasks for the task leaders easier. This system enhances, among employees, respect for each other, camaraderie and commitment that keeps the employee attrition rate below five percent (S. Mohapatra, personal communication, January 12, 2006). Similarly different organisations carry out different strategies for utilizing the informal communication network in the organisation. This they do because they understand the importance of "grapevine" or informal communication network for running the organisation smoothly.

Unfortunately, not all organisations have thought in terms of harnessing the "rumour mill" (Kalvar, 2005). Even though researches have proved that people at workplace spend *25% to 70% in face-to-face conversations, and about 88% to 93% in unscheduled communication (Whittaker et al., 1994),* organisations tend to remain prejudiced against informal communication. Most of the people in the top management feel that informal communication is a time-killing strategy of non-workers; informal communication is gossip and spreads rumours. Hence, we find in-house spying, nepotism, carrying-tails etc. becoming very common practices in organisations.

However, they sideline the merits of informal communication, which if handled strategically, can lead to non-distorted and quick dissemination of information. Frowning at informal communication goes against any natural law as the very origin of informal communication is due to the human tendency to talk and to form social hierarchies. Does that mean informal communication should be accepted the way it originates and operates in an organisation? What if the informal communication leads to group politics or individual victimization? Is there any other way to handle informal communication? Well, to find a solution to these questions, we need to briefly look at the concept of informal communication.

"Informal communication is called 'grapevine'. This type of communication arises on account of informal relationship between persons concerned. Informal communication grows spontaneously from personal and group interest, is characterized and may be conveyed by a simple glance, nod, smile, gesture and even mere silence. Informal channel is the most effective one and transmits information with considerable speed" (Rayadu 365). This informal communication operates in the organisation as a network on a non-official (hierarchies or formalities may not count much) basis yet, most of the time official matters are discussed and decisions are taken. The characteristics of an informal communication network are:

- There is no permanent structure
- It suggests how communication networks actually work
- It can route around to damage formal communication network
- It is situational and spontaneous
- It creates an organizational structure of its own

Informal communication comes into play between people due to proximity, perception of each other as a reliable or knowledgeable member, and friendship or trust. "Grapevine" in an organization is important because without grapevine employees cannot fill in gaps left from official word; they may not feel ownership of information. Through informal communication, employees can vent out their feelings, develop sense of belonging and discuss concerns off the records. Management can also learn what employees think in non-formal ways, which they cannot learn through formal networks. However, there are certain pitfalls of grapevine like unsubstantiated rumours that create dysfunction, incomplete rumours that propagate guess-work to substitute missing information, lack of secrecy and danger of confidential information leaking out, and dissemination of inaccurate information.

Rumours, generally, spread due to ambiguity of message and credibility of the transmitters. People believe rumours that involve those about whom they are curious to listen, if the message sounds important, if the management is opaque, and the information received through the rumour mill is timely and much awaited. The distortions in grapevine are due to condensation (reduction of details because all the information cannot be retained), information salience or sharpening (highlighting of key parts), closure or adding (filling in gaps to make information looks more credible) and selective perception of receiver.

Rayadu[6] suggests the following as the remedies to control rumours:

- To listen to the employees carefully and understand their mind.
- To have communication links with workers to keep a track of their events, activities, changes etc...
- To be honest and frank to enhance credibility and to promote confidence.
- To accommodate regular interactions with the key man or groups to learn people's reactions.
- To seek accurate answers and to disseminate exact information so that unsubstantiated talks are curbed.
- To have rumour control centres to facilitate anonymous reporting.

K. Davis offers the following solutions to contain spread of rumour:

- Remove causes of rumours.
- Apply efforts to serious rumours.
- Refute rumours with facts.
- Apply early effort to tackle rumours.
- Go for face-to-face dealings.
- Avoid repeating rumour while refuting.

– Encourage informal leaders if they are cooperative.
– Listen to all the rumours to understand its meaning (qtd. in Rayadu, 1998).

With this backdrop, some organisations, to sound more open and communicative, have tried to work on employee comfort and motivation to minimise/ control the ill-effects of informal communication. The organisations like Infosys, NTPC, HSBC, Eli Lilly, and HDFC Bank follow transparency as a feature to motivate people in the organization to be positive at work. This enables the employees to have access to more information. And the information is not restricted to HR policies and systems. It covers business strategy and performance, financial and operating results and the competitive scenario. Some of these organisations have also introduced "employment value proposition" to measure effective employer brand. The key to effective employer brand communication, both internally and externally, is authenticity and credibility. Employers are beginning to recognise that in order to create a strong employer brand, it is essential to develop good people policies and to communicate these externally as well as internally (The Best Companies to Work for in India, 2005).

To win employee confidence, BPCL has gone for a people oriented restructuring that has unified inter-linkages. As a manager says, "The old commandant rule is gone and it is now more a team based organization. There is lot more flexibility; it is like running your territory as your own business. It means I can do things differently, take risks, experiment and innovate" (Som, 2005). And NIIT encourages employees to find a marriage partner within the organization (... attract the best people, and they should make the best partners too) and offers the couple two months basic salary as gift apart from interest-free loans (Herr, 2005). It is well known that Maruti Udyog has tried to copy the Japanese management ethos. When it introduced a common canteen a few years ago, it was considered revolutionary. But today, argues R. Vasudevan its DGM Personnel in a new company, the same step would be received in a more matter of fact manner. The standard uniform code (grey) also prevails, which makes the employees equal and which is the first, external symbol of a flat organization. The lower you are in an organization, the higher the sense of satisfaction about commonality says Vasudevan. Similarly, everybody, bar none, punches in the morning and punches out at the end of the shift (Herr, 2005). Even in the UK, the organisations that want to keep people related problems at bay, implement HR practices that ultimately bring down rumours and distorts in "grapevine". For instance, Astron Group follows a philosophy of total involvement and celebration with customer-centric project teams in a problem-solving yet fun-filled and collaborative environment. St. Lukes Communications fosters and tries sustaining a powerfully creative culture with an 'equity-based' philosophy; using culture development tools, such as an 'organic' organisational structure, trust through communication, and formalised sharing (UK Best Places to Work, 2005).

Although organisations are trying to bring down the ill effects of informal communication by creating a more trustworthy, open and friendly culture, yet most of them have actually not addressed the informal communication network in its original form. For example, a survey conducted among the alumni of Institute of Management & Information Science, Bhubaneswar (working executives in different organisations in India), revealed that the reason for inducing a transparent or information sharing culture in the organisation tends to reflect HR motives more than organisational communication practices. Similarly, another opinion is that the efforts related to bring about fun and relaxation in the organisation may not help rearranging informal groups. In almost all the answers informal communication was a combination of unplanned, friendly and relaxing interaction that helped faster dissemination and gathering of information, building rapport, getting rid of stress and quick decision making. In the light of the answers collected from the sample, perhaps there is a need to reconsider the elements that constitute informal communication, and redefine them to make informal communication or "grapevine" more acceptable.

Owing to the reasons it comes into play the existence of informal communication in an organisation is but natural. For example, a manager is walking along the company corridor when he chances upon another manager, they greet, exchange pleasantries, discuss certain departmental issues and depart. After they reach their chambers both translate the discussion into action. In this case, the managers did not have a planned meeting, neither was the place meant for such discussions. In fact, both the managers were off to attend some other work nevertheless they utilized the chance meeting to exchange their personal and professional views. Finally, they converted the discussion to decision. This is a common practice in the organisations. However, there is less or no accountability associated with this kind of communication unless the communicators are committed to their exchange.

A research study conducted by Ellen Isaacs, Steve Whittaker, David Frohlich, and Brid O'Conaill (2005) has provided new taxonomy to types of informal communication:

(a) **Scheduled:** Meetings that are planned in advance by both parties.

(b)I **ntended:** Interactions that occur when one person seeks out another to discuss a specific topic, but where there is no pre-arranged plan to talk.

(c) **Opportunistic:** Interactions that occur when one person happens to see another and remembers that they wanted to discuss a particular topic with them.

(d)S **pontaneous:** Interactions that occur because two people happen to see each other and get into a conversation on a topic not prepared by either person.

They have identified the characteristics of informal communication as:

A short opportunistic interaction

Richard is standing up reading a document behind his desk when his colleague Frank walks into view on his way to his own desk from another office.

1. R: Frank can you read this report for me?
2. F: Now?
3. R: Aye if you've got a minute.
4. F: Yeah !

This interaction is completed in eight seconds. Richard sees that Frank is moving around the office and hence is not currently engaged in work, so he opportunistically solicits Frank's help. The shared visual environment affords Richard this information about Frank's availability and allows Frank and Richard to look at, and then physically exchange the document. The interaction is brief and has no formal openings or closings, such as greetings or farewells.

The following interaction shows an unplanned conversation between Richard and Frank that occurred immediately after Frank had finished a phone call to a client. It arose because Richard heard Frank's phone call and opportunistically monitored the outcome. It continues with Richard offering unprompted advice and assistance.

Frank is on the phone across the office from Richard. Frank puts down phone.

1. R: Is he alright?
2. F: Yeah.

3. R: Which one's he's got? There's a restaurant.
4. F: I said that I'll do this one initially and then further afield
5. R: Which one's that?
6. F: That's eighty, two Whiteladies road, it's the offices.
7. R: Oh, yeah we act for the landlord on that one. I did a rent review against him on that.
8. F: Right ().
9. R: His shop it might be worth checking out he's got a sub-tenant downstairs who's got a clothes shop
10. F: Yeah
11. R: Might be worth trying to get in with them as well.
12. F: Yeah, alright.

Again the interaction begins without formal initiation. The interaction has a history, revealed by the implicit shared context between the participants. Without being told, Richard knows the identity of Frank's caller (Line1), and details of the case (Line3). The shared context results in a condensed and cryptic conversational style. Towards the end of the fragment, Richard offers unprompted advice to Frank (Line12), which eventually results in an agreed action for Frank to report back (not shown). Thus, an unplanned conversation led to a detailed task-oriented discussion.

Their research adds on to say that Informal communication is vital for achieving certain types of work-related tasks. This happens because of physical proximity. Physical proximity promotes frequent, impromptu face-to-face communications, which are crucial for the planning and negotiation phases of projects (Finholt et al, 1990; Galegher et al, 1990, qtd. in Ellen Issacs, 2005). According to other research works there are negative impacts on teamwork when opportunities for ad hoc communication are reduced, as in remote collaboration. Work becomes more difficult to coordinate and advance despite the use of longer and more task-focused meetings in remote settings (Kraut et al, 1990 qtd. in Ellen Issacs, 2005).

In tandem to the findings of the survey **(Annexure I)** conducted among the alumni of Institute of Management & Information Science, Issacs' research also quotes research works that suggest that people in the workplace do not recognise value of informal communication. Kraut & Streeter (1995) found that impromptu communication is under-utilised compared with its value, whereas formal communication techniques are overused relative to their value. Most of the people admit that most of their work-related news and information come from informal interactions. In fact, informal communication can facilitate achieving organisational goals because it contributes to both social and production function of a group; the social function includes both member support (e.g. making sure people feel their contributions are valued) and group maintenance functions (e.g. keeping people informed of others' activities and ensuring that the groups' contributions are coordinated to achieve a common goal) (McGrath, 1991 qtd. in Ellen Issacs, 2005).

Now that the importance of harnessing grapevine has been established, it is pertinent to find a path to use it for facilitating right information, reducing organisational rumours and politics, and to make it a supportive tool for formal communication in the organisation. But before that, here are some suggestions (Kalvar, 2005) for making formal communication more reliable and effective so that informal communication does not become all pervasive:

– To ensure that individual reputation in the company adds weight to the communications. This is important because generally persons who are liked and admired are not misquoted. This can be done by avoiding some of the basic pitfalls of corporate communications like being clear in meaning, acknowledging uncertainty, and, when necessary, admitting mistake in public (if wrong).

– The second technique requires the use of exchange of information to individual's advantage. This can be done by carefully seeding select information into the network, placing it where it is most likely to reach the right ears. To do this, it has to be determined, who is the target for the information? Who is the target most likely to turn to in order to find out the information? How can we seed the information we want passed on?

Building credibility in the formal communications and leveraging the informal communications channel enable the organisation to turn the corporate social network to its advantage. Since, strengthening of formal network has already been discussed; we need to find a system to leverage the informal communication network.

This paper suggests an "open eye and ear approach" to managerial communication that would facilitate harnessing the strength of grapevine. What is "open eye and ear approach" and how does it work? "Open eye and ear approach" is a communicative approach that advocates keen observation and empathic listening in managerial communication that can exploit the potential of informal communication. Being a communicative approach, it focuses on *individual capability enhancement*, thus, making the whole approach, a communication skill- a skill that uses eyes and ears for deciphering codes. The *individual capability* in this approach is not that of the sender, but is of the *receiver*. There is a total reversal in the normal communication process. The manager/ executive is the receiver and the communication process is *sender-centred* i.e., the sender can frame the message as he/ she likes. But the receiver should be communicatively competent to decipher the truth in the message. In this approach receiver also ensures that all information reaches him/ her. Therefore, the receiver in this approach should possess *receiving skills and deciphering skills.*

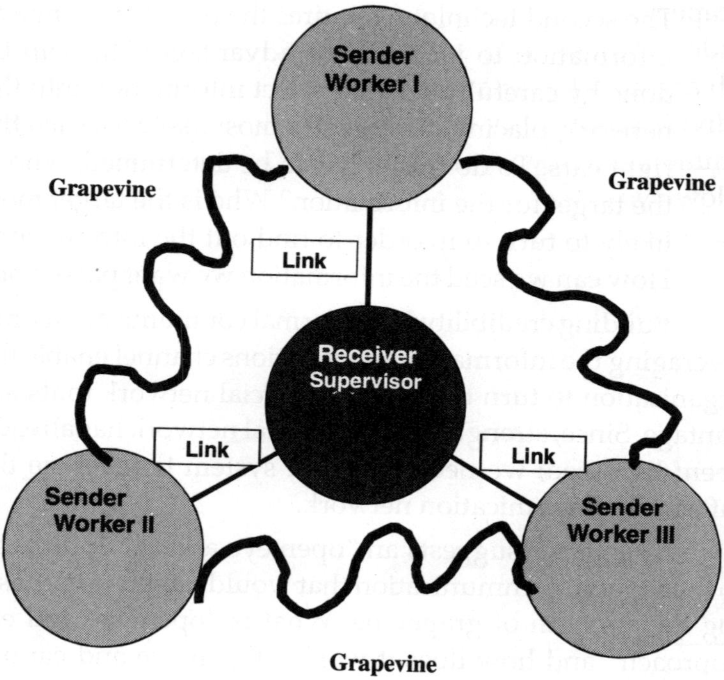

Most of the communication wizards recommend a receiver-centred approach to communication. Aristotle, in his model of communication, advises the speaker on constructing a speech for different audiences on different occasions for different effects. While Laswell's model talks of "effect", Shannon and Weaver's model emphasises "transmission of messages". Chomsky insists on an ideal native speaker-hearer pair, and Hymes advocates speaker's communicative competence. Individual capability enhancement addresses the need to improve listening skills, probing skills, decoding shibboleth, utterance analysis skills, and skills to respond strategically. In this approach, receiver ensures that all information reaches him or her. Therefore, the receiver in this approach should possess *receiving skills and deciphering skills.*

Receiving skills include establishing links with all the informal groups operating in the organisation so that no *talk* escapes the ears, and no *act* the *eyes*. Deciphering skills include observing, reading body language, decoding shibboleth and finding out missing links. These skills will lead to individual capability enhancement to effectively handle the communication network in the organisation. It works in the following way:

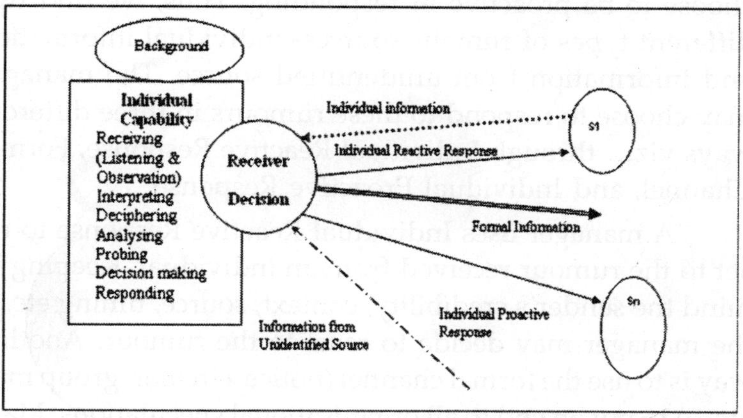

This illustration shows how the individual capability of a receiver enhances effective responses. The background of the receiver includes experience, knowledge, culture, faith, belief, trust, attitude, personal attributes etc... The background influences the receiver's individual capability and the channel of receipt of information. Each piece of information generates a different decision that leads to an individual response. While the decision relates to finding out true or invented categories, responses relate to the communicative act between the sender and the receiver.

The diagram is a depiction of what actually happens in an organisation. There are many employees in an organisation say S1 to Sn. All the employees do not spread rumours. Some carry rumours forward to the higher levels, some others keep it within their group, and others are unaware of these rumours. There are basically different ways to address these rumours. For instance, when S1 comes with unsubstantiated information, the manager's individual capability and background help him/her to take a decision. This decision can be an individual reactive response or information transmission through "formal" channel. Sometimes some individuals are unaware of the corporate politics that operates around them. In such cases, manager may choose to be proactive in responding. Thus, we find two different types of rumour sources- individual information and information from unidentified source. The manager may choose to respond to these rumours in three different ways viz... through Individual Reactive Response, Formal Channel, and Individual Proactive Response.

A manager uses Individual Reactive Response to react to the rumour received from an individual. Keeping in mind the sender's credibility, context, source, timing etc..., the manager may decide to react to the rumour. Another way is to use the formal channel (notice, circular, group mail etc...) to put an end to all organisational speculations. Manager may do this to put an end to negative rumours related to issues like pay hike, bonus, lay-off etc... Such use of formal channel helps bringing down the anxiety of employees. It may sometimes even warn gossipers to keep away from spreading false stories. At times, manager may act based on information received from unknown sources to inform, convince, persuade, direct, or warn individual as a proactive measure. This may be to curb individual victimisation or to warn an individual.

The links used to gather information can be established in different ways. The manager or executive could become the "key person" of every informal group and tap the grapevine. They could also become a "god father (mother)" by nurturing individuals/ groups, and in turn, gathering all information. They could become "detached intruders" who would not react to any information or informal talk. They could also use a third party "intervention" like a consultant or a counsellor *(See annexure II)*.

All these communication styles help tapping the potential of informal communication because unlike formal channel of communication. Since, proximity increases, trust and relationship strengthen. And the chances of spreading rumours and making organisational politics reduce. Well, this is not just applicable to the head or the team leader. Any individual who wants to exploit communication potential of an organisation to its fullest capacity can use this approach. He/ She can also facilitate spontaneous discussions during informal meetings to encourage free talk and brainstorming. Inducing humour during informal communication sessions can help develop creativity, and can reduce stress levels at work place.

The use of a consultant also helps. A mobile service providing organisation in Bhubaneswar was used for experimenting with the use of a third party intervention for tapping informal communication. The consultant's job for a month was only to talk to the call-centre executives. The talk included both job performance and social norms. 95% of the executives shared information with the consultant, which was then used to create a more cooperative work environment.

This approach can be included in the managerial communication curriculum to help the budding managers become a skilful receiver as well. The course may include:

— Informal Communication- An overview.

— Types of informal communication- Based on people involved, information transfer process and opportunistic approaches.

— Importance of informal communication.

— When does informal communication fail?

– Harnessing the "rumour mill".
– The open eye and ear approach- the sender-centred approach.
– Communication skills needed to control informal communication.
– Practice exercises.

This course intends to hone the following skills of the participants:

– Active Listening & Empathy.
– Utterance Analysis Observation.
– Reading non-verbal cues.
– Decoding shibboleth.
– Finding missing links.
– Reading between lines.
– Human Relations.
– Strategic linguistic competence.

In fact, this can also help the executives prepare themselves well for the corporate informal communication. It can help them convert the inevitable harsher realities of organisational communication to unending pleasant exchanges.

REFERENCES

1. Business Today, November 20, 2005, The best companies to work for in India, Retrieved December 26, 2005 from http://www.aspiresys.com/web_pages/business_today/business_today.htm
2. Davis, K., Human Behaviour at Work, Tata McGraw Hill Publishing Company, New Delhi (quoted in Rayadu) p.389
3. Herr, Harveen , The New Corporate Mantra, Retrieved December 29, 2005 from http://lifepositive.com/
4. Issacs, Ellen and others, Informal communication re-examined: New functions for video in supporting opportunistic encounters, Lawrence Erlbaum book, Video-Mediated Communication, 1994, p. 459-485 Retrieved December 30,2005, from http://izix.com/

5. Kalvar, Shannon T., Harness the power of the informal communications network. Retrieved December 20, 2005 from http://techrepublic.com.com/5100-10878-5092209-1.html

6. Management From Out Front: A Workplace Catches Up to The Work.. Retrieved December 26, 2005 from http://www.steelcase.com/na/knowledgedesign.aspx?f=10259&c=10977

7. Rayadu, C.S, Communication, Himalaya Publishing House, New Delhi, 1998, p.388

8. Som, Ashok, Organisational Redesign at BPCL: The Challenge of Privatisation, Retrieved December 26, 2005 from Som_ Organizational% 20Redesign%20at%20BPCL% 20The %20Challenge% 20of% 20Priva %E2%80%A6

9. UK best work places Retrieved December 29, 2005 from http://www.best-practice.com/

ANNEXURE- I : QUESTIONNAIRE (WITH RESULTS)

Name: Organisation:

Designation:

Please place a tick mark against the item(s) you find appropriate:

1. Transparent and information sharing management tries to induce-
   a. Positive HR culture **(40%).**
   b. Bring down rumours emerging from informal communication **(26%).**
   c. Make HR strategies useful for work **(32%).**
   d. Want to empower employees **(2%).**
2. Fun in the organisation -
   a. Reduces stress **(60%).**
   b. Develops commitment to the organisation **(20%).**
   c. Helps rearranging informal groups **(4%).**
   d. Helps communicating with even those you may not like **(16%).**
3. At the work place most of the communication takes place through –
   a. Formal network (pre-planned with agenda distributed etc...).
   b. Informal network (spontaneous or as and when needed) **(100%).**
4. Informal Communication is –
   a. Unplanned communication.
   b. Friendly communication.
   c. Talking for relaxation.
   d. All the above **(100%).**
5. Informal Communication helps –
   a. Faster dissemination and gathering of information.

b. Building rapport.
c. Getting rid of stress.
d. Quick decision making.
e. All the above **(100%)**.

ANNEXURE- II : THREE ROLE-BASED STYLES FOR HARNESSING INFORMAL COMMUNICATION

Key Person Style

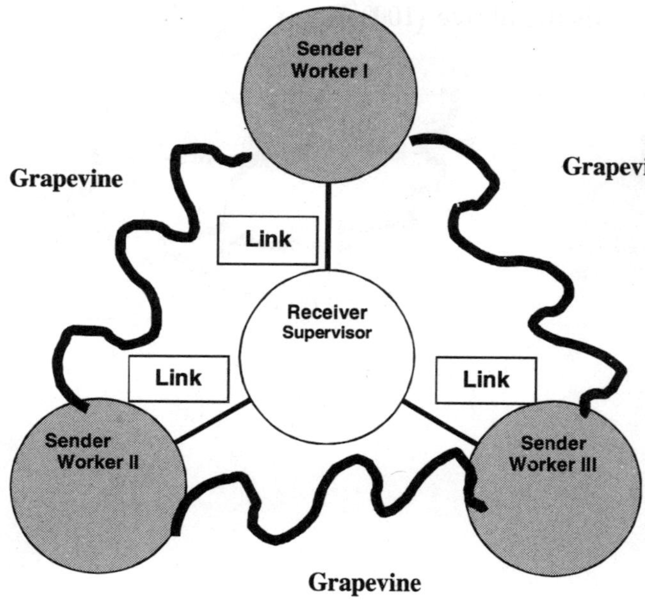

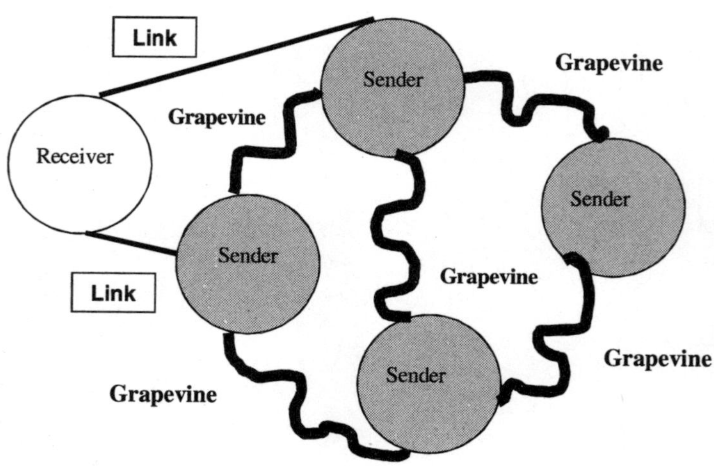

Third-Party Intervention

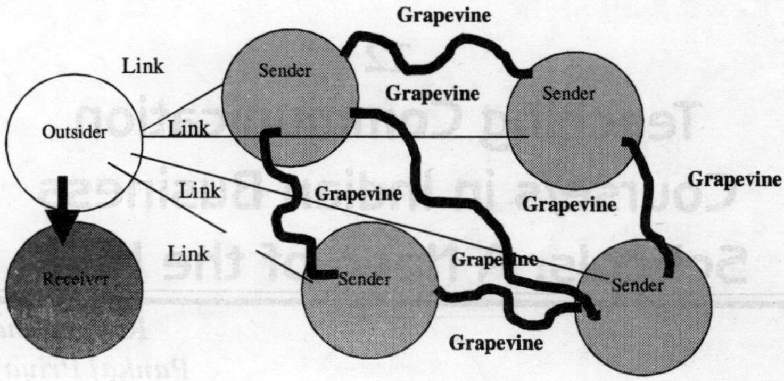

12

Teaching Communication Course/s in Indian Business Schools: A Need of the Hour

*R. L. Raina**
*Pankaj Priya***

ABSTRACT

Communication is the lifeline of any individual or organization if it wants to excel in today's world. Hence, it has been incorporated in one form or the other in almost all leading Business Schools. However, still the teaching of this discipline is not receiving adequate thrust and attention it deserves in good number of schools. An attempt has already been taken to understand as to how this discipline is handled in top ranking Business Schools in NCR Region.

KEYWORDS : Communication, Business Communication.

INTRODUCTION

Communication courses are an inherent part of any Business School curriculum. Yet, it has received step motherly treatment from the designers of the course - curriculum. It has not been scientifically designed and produced in a need based format in Indian Business schools. The repercussions of this lackadaisical approach are manifested in the poor performance of the students when

* Professor Communications Area, LBSIM, Delhi

** Faculty, Marketing Area, LBSIM, Delhi

they enter the corporate world.

OBJECTIVE

- To find out the level of existence of communication course in Indian Business Schools.
- To analyze the topics covered in the courses being taught in the Business schools.
- To find the teaching pedagogy followed in these Business schools.

RESEARCH METHODOLOGY

The research is an empirical study based on primary research which was conducted through a structured questionnaire (Appendix 1) circulated among fifteen business schools in NCR, Delhi. Where ever the information was available on the website of these concerned Institute, the relevant information was taken care of..

FINDINGS

- All the fifteen Business Schools have a course on Business Communication in their curriculum.
- All the fifteen Business Schools have an independent Business Communication Course.
- Twelve Schools have a full credit course and Three Schools have two half Credit course extending over two trimesters.
- All Respondents agreed that this course has been in existence since the launch of the MBA program in their Institute.
- Topics covered in this course are similar in Nature but with varying emphasis on different areas.
- Two Institutes have trained Faculty devoted to this area.
- Two Institutes have visiting Faculty for this area.

- Eleven Institutes involve faculty from other discipline to teach this course.
- Teaching Pedagogy consists of Lectures and Exercise.
- Four Institutes admitted that they also incorporate Role-play and Audio Visual Media in their course curriculum.
- All respondents rated it as an important course.
- Feedback from their alumni / Corporate – The level of communication needs improvement.

LIMITATIONS

Sample Size is small and restricted to NCR Delhi.

The respondents did not answer some of the questions properly.

Since the Questionnaire was emailed, some of the respondents may have interpreted it in some other manner leading to bias.

CONCLUSION

Despite incorporating Business communication in the course curriculum, Business Schools have failed to give due importance to this course which is very much reflected in the availability of trained faculty for this course and the teaching pedagogy adopted in the Institutes.

13

An Evaluative Study of 'Business Communication' Courses Taught in Leading U.S./ UK/European Business Schools A Proposal

*R .L. Raina**

ABSTRACT

It is an admitted fact that the treatment given to teaching course/s in the area of "Businesses Communication" in Indian b-schools, even among some of the top ones, is not on expected lines. The results, therefore, are not comparable to the b-schools graduates of the western world, particularly in the context of US, UK and Europe. Industry and recruiter perception and feedback is also on similar lines. Our boys and girls, bright young management graduates, are good in concepts, techniques and so on but lack decidedly when it comes to making the most of what they know using their communication skills. To address this question, the paper makes a case for studying the ways of handling the teaching of the course/s in the area of business communication at some of the benchmarked schools abroad, particularly in terms of course content, pedagogy, evaluation mechanism and feedback process.

* Professor, Communications Area and Director, Lal Bahadur Shastri Indistitute of Management, Delhi.

INTRODUCTION

A recent survey (Feb. - June, 2000) undertaken by IIM Lucknow, to seek industry/alumni input/feedback for restructuring its course curriculum, revealed that the course/s taught in the area of Communication needed to be reworked upon, particularly in terms of content delivered, pedagogy followed and the assessment and evaluation techniques used. Similar revelations came up, in more concrete terms, in AMDISA Workshop (June 2000) on 'Reinventing Management Education' as well as in IIM Ahmedabad 'National Seminar on Teaching Business Communication at Indian Business Schools' (March 2001).

OBJECTIVES

Recognizing the importance of Communication in highly competitive global economies, and appreciating the fact that the communication courses/programs in the US business schools, have evolved over a period of time, the basic thrust should be to examine how this discipline is handled in leading business schools in the US.

PROBLEM AREAS FOR INVESTIGATION

In the context of global and multicultural business environment, communication problems of professionals assume great importance. Therefore, in a management school, developing abilities of effective communication in students is a major concern. 'Communication', thus, is a very important module. It prepares the students to excel in whatever they do by teaching them to express and advocate ideas effectively, and to understand and appreciate the diversity of human communication practices. The 'course inputs' help students develop and refine their 'communication' skills in various spheres, including communication in inter-personal, inter-group and inter-organizational relationships. The critical question, therefore, is how do we go about developing and delivering course inputs, which would be of significance and of value addition in respect of their current and future professional career.

At broader levels, the students must also study communication climates and cultures, emergent networks, information environments, organizational symbols, information technologies, and cross-cultural communication in corporate settings. They must also understand the impact of messages transmitted by various mass media, role of communication in the functioning of complex organizations. The courses must also address issues such as target group analysis, internal/external communication integration, systems analysis and channel effectiveness. Again, the question is how do we go about incorporating such inputs in the course curriculum and delivering the same.

Use of 'technology' in 'communication' is another area that needs to be comprehensively understood and investigated. Communication with new technologies is of great importance to students as they enter organizations in various capacities. This would include an understanding of the technologies and the effects of technology usage, theories of media choice and usage, implementation and adoption of communication technology in organizations. A special mention must be made here of the specific communication technologies (including Internet and intranets, WWW, email, computer conferencing, videoconferencing, electronic meeting systems, voice mail, pagers, fax, speech recognition, etc.) used in organizations.

HYPOTHESIS TO BE TESTED

Effective management of 'communication' helps businesses grow and be more competent and competitive. This would be tested through the survey and interaction based research component of the study, which will focus on understanding US academic/industry perception about the courses/programmes handled in the area.

RESEARCH METHODS & APPROACHES

The research approach would focus on both, academic as well as industry perspectives. In order to assess the industry needs, a select group of US industries would be approached to complete a questionnaire, designed for the purpose, to bring out those aspects of 'Communication', which are of particular help for the business to grow. Interviewing a cross section of industrial houses will further back this up and authenticate the findings.

Similarly, questionnaires would also be administered to the teachers and students of select business schools to highlight academic perspectives as to the need fulfillment. This two-pronged approach will, in the ultimate analysis, help us to: (i) understand relevance of the course contents, pedagogy followed, assessment/evaluation techniques adopted, etc.; (ii) identify strengths as well as gaps; and (iii) design, develop, and deliver need based courses/programs.

This study reinforced by mutually complimentary aspects of theory and practice, will go a long way to bridge the gap and develop and deliver state-of-the-art courses in the discipline.

RESEARCH DONE IN THE AREA

So far as work done by other scholars in the area is concerned, reference can be made to the following works:

- **Wardrope and Bayless :** Content of the Business Communication Course. Business Communication Quarterly 62(4)1999: 33-40.
- **Murranka and Lynch :** Developing a Competency Based Fundamentals of Management Communication Course. Business Communication Quarterly 62(3)1999: 9-23.

– **Knight** : Management Communication in US MBA Programs. Business Communication Quarterly 62(4)1999: 9-32.

RELEVANCE OF THE WORK TO INDIA

As illustrated earlier, incorporation of 'Communication' courses in the MBA curriculum in India is of recent origin. There is obviously scope for strengthening them vis-à-vis industries' requirements, particularly at a time when the economy of India is taking the path to globalization. Indian Institute of Management Lucknow is in the forefront in the context of offering courses in 'Business Communication'. The proposed study would go a long way in bringing state-of-the-art in the curricula at the Institute and thereby giving it an opportunity to lead the rest in the country. Further, American experiences will also enable us to develop and conduct a series of workshops for teachers of Indian business schools, involved in handling 'Communication' courses. In addition, my interaction with the academics there will be of immense help to me in organizing a series of innovative workshops and management development/training programs, in the area, for the corporate leaders, back home.

JUSTIFICATION FOR UNDERTAKING THE STUDY

Some of the lead business schools in the US/UK/ Europe have been quite successful in giving a scientific treatment to the study of communication through extensive research and close interaction between the academics and industry. The wealth of information available from the research in (and teaching of) this discipline could, therefore, be of enormous value to the business schools in India, particularly keeping in mind that India is at the threshold of globalization.

Given the experience of US/UK/European industry in global business, it is perhaps natural that 'Communication Courses' are that much more vibrant in the business schools over there. To get the best out of the proposed study, visits to some of the leading business schools and industrial houses in those contexts would be of help to gain first hand knowledge through personal interaction. I strongly believe that there can hardly be any other substitute to this.

14

Technology Implications in Professional Communication

*Susheel Chhabra**

ABSTRACT

Effective communication in professional as well as personal life has become an essential ingredient for success. The most important requirements for effective communication are personalization, handling e-mail effectively, security of communication, user's training, and availability of Information & Communication Technologies (ICTs) infrastructure. Professional communication in this dynamic electronic environment requires effective planning and well designed guidelines. The paper discusses some useful software to achieve personalization at workplace along with guidelines for online communication. The basic objective is to learn how technology implications can be converted into positive strengths for communicating professionally.

KEYWORDS : Professional Communication, Information & Communication Technologies (ICTs), Technology, Implications, Personalisation.

INTRODUCTION

Information and Communication Technologies (ICTs) are contributing significantly to enhance the quality of communication. In professional communication, communicator's objective is to portray the document or

* Faculty, IT Area, Lal Bahadur Shastri Institute of Management, Delhi

verbal message to successfully reveal the meaning in a concise and logical manner. Global projects using Networks computing for distance communication and coordination are becoming popular. As a result, team members are often located geographically apart, while working towards a common project goal (Lee-Kelley, 2006).

Electronic collaboration has also become a driver for productivity as organizations develop linkages for the planning, sourcing, and execution of goods and services around the world (Qureshi, Sajda & Keen, Peter, 2005). Web and video conferencing brings a new way of communicating with coworkers. Unlike an in-person conference, web and video-based meetings are easy to save and store real-time. The participants can review material easily and can analyze how the presentation went. It is a convenient and cost-effective way to collaborate and plan projects. These tools are also valuable for improving intercultural and online communication skills of people from various cultures around the world (Elisabeth, 2006).

The implications of technology for professional communication can have far reaching consequences if not handled properly. Recently published research evidence suggests that whilst video conferencing and other advanced information and communication technologies have various capabilities, successes in their application may be short lived and modest in achievement (Bower, D.J., Hinks, J., Wright, H., Hardcastle, C. & Cuckow, H., 2001). The following sections discuss the implications of technology along with suitable measures, for effective professional communication.

PERSONALIZATION IN THE WORKPLACE

As companies start using web or video conferencing to communicate with each other, people have to get used to talking with people via computer screens and microphones. People may act and speak differently when looking at a computer screen than they would if they were in a face-to-face interaction. They may not catch the communicator's underlying meanings. This requires personalization of audience experiences. The level of personalization in the workplace depends on the context, emotional support, expressions, trust, and situation of the environment. The personalization in the workplace can be achieved by creating relationships that enhance the effectiveness of the information needed for documents.

Some conferencing software allows for integrated audio and video communications to make presentations more dynamic. This helps to enhance the degree of personalization in the workplace. Communication software can help to edit and discuss documents through application or screen sharing tools. That way everyone who is working on the project or who has a stake in it is able to have input in each step of its creation.

Applications for instant real time communication are growing more popular in the business world. America Online this week released a corporate version of its popular instant messenger. Yahoo! launched a corporate messaging application last month, and Microsoft is working on software, code-named Greenwich, designed for internal corporate messaging. IBM already sells a business product called 'Sametime'.

Microsoft's NetMeeting is the most popular one to personalize the meeting experience in a conference. It provides video and audio conferencing, chat, Internet directory, file transfer, program sharing, remote desktop sharing and whiteboard facility. Live meeting makes it easier to schedule sessions, invite attendees, and host interactive sessions.

While hosting a live meeting, attendees receive personalized invitations with a unique meeting URL and password. When meeting is set to begin, participants browse through the URL and sign in. If they have not attended a live meeting session before, the required software is installed automatically.

Fig. 1. Microsoft's NetMeeting

Fig. 2. Microsoft's NetMeeting Interactive Sessions

Live Meetings are fully interactive and collaborative. Live Meeting lets us review, annotate, and discuss any printable file, including Microsoft Office PowerPoint, Word, and Excel files, as well as PDFs. Also, one can conduct real-time polls, share applications, and collaborate by using a whiteboard.

PROFESSIONALISM IN E-MAIL COMMUNICATION

The way people communicate via e-mail is very important. The e-mail is used to communicate with audience, submit documents and discuss information online. The communicators must always treat the audience with the same professionalism in e-mail as they do in face-to-face encounters.

We are now in an information chaos situation. Especially e-mail overload directly affects individuals' stress levels, as well as the amount of time spent managing e-mails. Constant stress from this e-mail overload has led to mental fatigue. Subsequently, office hours are increasing, cutting into personal time, productivity is falling, and companies are losing money.

People tend to be more informal in e-mail messages; This can alter a relationship. Communicators should adhere to basic etiquette for online communication. The messages should be brief and to the point, the comments or questions should be limited to the subject of the mail. The subject line plays a very important role in communication. It is an identifier that provides a brief summary of what an e-mail message is about. Composing a good subject line is important and helps us and others sort, manage, and filter e-mail. The subject line should be logical and concise and should cover the essence of the message. By effectively utilizing the subject line, the body of the message can be shortened to a significant extent. Use of signature files to identify correspondence and contact information in an e-mail can save significant time of the communicator.

'COOKIES' AND THEIR EFFECT ON PROFESSIONAL COMMUNICATION

Some organizations try to personalize the audience experience while they surf the Internet by using "Cookie". Amazon.com is one of the examples. When we visit a website, the company whose website we are accessing may store our personal information on their server and place a text file on our computer to track us through the cookies. With most Internet browsers, we can erase "Cookies" from our computer hard drive, block all "Cookies", or receive a warning before a "Cookie" is stored. The cookies can be the main source of stealing the privacy of individuals and companies on the Internet.

INFORMATION ACCESS AND AVAILABILITY OF INFRASTRUCTURE FOR PROFESSIONAL COMMUNICATION

Organizations are also struggling with the balance of securing data while providing adequate access to information for efficiency. The challenge is in ensuring that only authorized users have access to business-critical data. Without accurate detection, employees must fight a sea of inefficient policies and barricades just to get their job done. And without appropriate security, the sensitive information that should be facilitating efficiency may actually become a security hazard. So, there is a need to train the organizations as how to protect information and ensure data privacy.

As the use of technology is increasing in professional communication, there is a need to have availability of technology infrastructure the availability of infrastructure will boost the trust level of communicators and audience and they can depend on the technology fearlessly.

Significant amount of investment is required to establish, implement and maintain the technological tools for effective communication. Sometimes, it has been seen that after investing so much in hardware, organizations feel shy to invest in software. The software plays an important role in providing secure and sound infrastructure. The return on investment from technology infrastructure as demanded by the management can only be achieved by effective use of technology.

EFFECTIVE PLANNING FOR COMMUNICATING ONLINE

Planning ahead can help to avoid straying from goals or a set agenda. Selecting a location plays an important role in effective communication.

> The location should be selected where an audio-video conference won't be disturbed. Encourage teleconferencing participants to use the mute option on their phone when they aren't speaking. While moderating the call, invite others to speak in order to establish a level of interaction. Follow up after the conference call with minutes of the meeting or a summary of decisions to keep everyone apprised of what happened.

More and more people are using discussion and chat tools for professional communication. These communications may be synchronous (in real time) or asynchronous (at varied times). The communicator should not forget that he/she is speaking to a group; if there is a need to reply or respond to an individual, it should be done privately. The information should be posted in a timely manner and meaningful replies should carry the conversation forward.

The training of the users in the use and maintenance of technology is very important for effective communication. The learning of technology by the users is not an easy task, which requires a constant practice to become familiar with. On an average it has been seen that it takes at least three (3) months to align employees with the new electronic communication tool. Some of the major guidelines for effective communication are given as under:

Guidelines for online communication

- Online communication should be conducted over a secure network, with provisions for authentication and encryption. Standard e-mail services do not meet these guidelines, so the user should be aware of potential security risks, including unauthorized physical access and security of computer hardware, and guard against them with technologies such as automatic logout and password protection.
- The communicator should take reasonable steps to authenticate the identity of correspondent(s) in an electronic communication and to ensure that recipients of information are authorized to receive it. The user also take reasonable steps to protect privacy.
- The use of online communications may increase the risk of unauthorized distribution of information and create a clear record of this distribution. The communicator must establish and follow procedures that help to mitigate this risk.
- Prior to the initiation of online communication, informed consent should be obtained regarding the appropriate use and limitations of this form of communication.
- Online interactions are subject to requirements of licensure. While communicating online outside the country in which the provider holds a license may subject the provider to increased risk.
- Web sites and online communications of an advertising, promotional or marketing nature may subject to increase liability, including implicit guarantees or implied warranty. Misleading or deceptive claims increase this liability.

CONCLUSION

The effective communication requires personalization at the workplace as face-to-face interaction has been considered as using best for professional communication. The personalization using automated mode requires human touch (body language, face expressions, eye contact, etc). By adhering to proper guidelines for professional communication in online environment, the positive effects of online communication can be harnessed. It has also been felt that while e-mail is an effective tool for professional communication, we still need to have proper etiquette to achieve success in communication. Although ICTs tools help achieve better communication, access control and availability of infrastructure are essential to achieve success.

REFERENCES

1. Bower, D.J., Hinks, J., Wright, H., Hardcastle, C. & Cuckow, H. (2001). Construction Innovation, 1(2).
2. Elisabeth, Gareis (2006). The Journal of Language for International Business. Glendale, 17(2).
3. http://www.microsoft.com/windows/NetMeeting/Features/default.ASP
4. http://www.som.cranfield.ac.uk/som/privacy.asp
5. Lee-Kelley, Liz (2006). Locus of control and attitudes to working in virtual teams. International Journal of Project Management,24(3).
6. Pratt, Andrew (2006). Email Overload in the Workplace: A Multi-Dimensional Exploration. Retrieved May 10, 2007 from http://orange.eserver.org/issues/5-1/pratt.html.
7. Qureshi, Sajda & Keen, Peter (2005). IEEE Transactions on Professional Communication. 48(1).
8. Whitehead, Bob (2005). Conferencing online versus face-to-face meetings. Retrieved November 14, 2006 from http://www.web-conferencing-zone.com/4051-conferencing-online.htm.

INDEX

Business Communication 211,212,59,60,70,75,77,79.
Business School Curriculum 40.
Communication 150,152,156,157,159,162.
Capability 199,201.
Development 157,159
Delivery 75.
Effective Communication 90,92,94,,95,97.
Evaluation 77,78,79,81
Forest and Natural Resource Management 158,159,167,168.
FTA (Face threatening Act) 118,119,12,123,124,125,126,128.
Feedback 62,64,67,68,77,78,79,81.
Horizontal Influence 118.
ICT 219,220,227
Implication 220
Interaction 192,195,196
Leadership Communication 91,93,94,95,100.
Learning 153,181.
Logos 93,96,100.
Managerial Persuasion 40,45,52
Management 158,162.
Persuasive Communication 40,42,46,47.
Pedagogy 47,77.
Pathos 93,98,100.
Professional Vcommunication 219,220,223,224,225,227.
Personalisation 221,227.
.Rumour Mill 190,204
Systematic Managerial Persuasion 53.
Upward Influence 118,119,120,122,123,124,125,126,127.
Vertical Influence 118
Written Analysis 152.